GIFTS
❧ *from your* ❧
KITCHEN

GIFTS
❧ *from your* ❧
KITCHEN

Creating and Packaging
Presents of Food
and Drink

SUSAN FRICK CARLMAN

CHICAGO
REVIEW
PRESS

Carlman, Susan F.
 Gifts from your kitchen : creating and packaging presents of food
and drink / Susan Frick Carlman. — 1st ed.
  p. cm.
 Includes index.
 ISBN 1-55652-191-X (pbk.) : $11.95
 1. Cookery. 2. Gifts. I. Title.
 TX652.C328 1993
 641.5—dc20   93-2359
                                                                              CIP

Interior illustrations by Ellen Dessloch

Cover Photograph: Tim Turner
Food Stylist: Irene Bertolucci
Style Assistants: Ellen Dessloch and Lisa Martiny

Published by Chicago Review Press, Incorporated
814 North Franklin Street
Chicago, Illinois, 60610

Printed in the United States of America

ISBN 1-55652-191-X

5 4 3 2 1

To Dan, Erin, Sam, and Molly,
whose love is the gift
that nourishes my soul

Contents

Introduction

It wasn't so much the baking that appealed to us—though certainly a day spent up to our elbows in flour and sugar held a certain attraction. And it wasn't exactly the sisterly camaraderie that made the annual ritual something to look forward to; we five girls generally spent as much time snarling at one another as purring in the blissful harmony of siblinghood. And you know what they say about crowded kitchens and too many cooks.

No, the annual holiday baking day held a separate magic all its own. We would go more or less amiably about our respective tasks, each of us assigned a cookie species or two. We'd work happily for hours under a light cloud of flour dust, content in the knowledge that at day's end we'd have all those festively cellophane-wrapped assortments of cookies tagged and ready to deliver. And we knew that, on opening this wondrous thing we had made, people would gasp and sigh and otherwise show us their utter delight. We knew this was so, because we knew Mom was right: the very best gifts are the ones you make yourself.

Gifts of food bring a special congeniality, a certain message that says, "I like you a lot, enough to make a delicious present for you." Because if Mom also was right when she said that it's the thought that counts—and after all, she was just about always right—then there probably is no more thoughtful gift you can give than a homemade one. And if moms were further right when they admonished (mine didn't do this one, but lots of

1

other moms did), "The way to a person's heart is through their stomach," then what more do you need to know?

On these pages we will look at ways to give foods, always with the sense that in both the cooking and the packaging it is good to express oneself, to come up with a pretty and delicious final product that reflects the giver and the giver's high regard for the recipient.

Sometimes gift foods are put up in jars, colorful jewels of sweet and savory treats that can enrich the pantry shelf with all their enticing promise until eating time comes. Sometimes they are bound up in bags, baskets, or boxes. There are lots of ways to give gifts of deliciousness, liquid and solid, from condiments to pastas, from the partly prepared (and ready to mix up fresh) to the ready to eat.

Similarly, there are a nearly infinite number of ways to present a present. Suggestions to send you off on your own packaging expedition will be found here—ideas for wrappings, trimmings, and labelings that I hope will enable you to develop your own style of packaging. Your family and friends will begin to recognize *your* kitchen's treasures as the most special of gifts, and they will come to anticipate them with great pleasure.

Most important, though, we'll celebrate the philosophy of giving, and all the deliciousness it can entail.

PART I

THE PRESENT-ATION

Just as important as the gift you give is the way you give it. How you say something generally is at least as important as what you actually say, and likewise the presentation of a homemade present is as much an expression of yourself as the food you have prepared. Of course the stuff will be delicious no matter how you pack it, but why not extend as far as possible the joy of receiving such a special thing? A carefully assembled outer covering makes the prize inside all the more enticing and a greater pleasure to receive.

This chapter offers ideas for packaging and presenting your culinary products, turning them into wonderful gifts to leave mysteriously on doorsteps, hand deliver to a party, place lovingly beneath the Christmas tree, pass out to departing tea party guests, and lovingly place in the hands of family and friends.

Once you start giving away your pretty packages of homemade food, you'll find there are numerous excuses and reasons for doing so, just as there are plenty of ways to make the presents look special. I confess I haven't got much step-one, step-two guidance for you. You won't find any predetermined packages here. (You know the sort of instructions I mean, as in "Go get this kind of jar, follow these 10 steps, look at photos 12A–12F, and you'll get exactly this undistinguished result.") I prefer instead to provide many ideas, in the hope you'll be inspired to choose among them to create gifts that reflect you, the giver. Your jars of chutney shouldn't look just like my jars of chutney, which shouldn't look just like my neighbor's. What, then, would be the pleasure of wrapping it up and giving it away? What then, would be the fun of sidestepping the expensive gourmet food shops for your own creative, more affordable efforts?

The emphasis in the title of this book, then, should be on the word *your,* for no other kitchen could produce that particular dressing or baking mix for those particular loved ones. In a world overwhelmed by the mass produced, the gifts from your kitchen should indeed be custom made.

So in the interests of personal expression and a commitment to good taste beyond the culinary kind, this section provides some ways to carry the made-this-just-for-you theme through to the presentation of the food, be it a container for a food, a carrier for several foods, or ideas for putting together your own distinctive vessels or gift wrapping. Remember, no gift is more deliciously thoughtful than that which you design and make yourself.

Vessels

The perfect vessel for your food might be as accessible as your kitchen cupboard. Like many cooks, you might have a copious stash of glass jars tucked away, and among them might be something that would suit that mustard or those nuts just right. Scrub it up, tie on a fresh trimming or two, and you're all set. Such is the spur-of-the-moment approach.

But, of course, there is also the more careful, thoughtful production of gift foods, and there are many possibilities for packaging. The number of ways in which you can wrap up your carefully made food is limited only by your imagination—and perhaps a few requirements set by the food itself. Liquids don't work well in cardboard boxes, for instance. I think it's always a good idea to look at the food and think carefully about how *best* to package it, what sort of container will keep it tasting its best, and go from there.

Reincarnated Containers

Of course, recycled items are among the most accessible, economical, and environmentally correct ways to package food gifts. It's a good idea, anyway, to get into the habit of saving wine bottles (keep the cork!), interesting jars, previously used crates (such as miniature fruit crates), gift tins, and the like. You never know when you'll find the perfect use for such things. Even things like reasonably attractive covered plastic tubs and those cylindrical containers that oatmeal and cornmeal come in can be saved to be decorated and reincarnated for giving things like dry mixes and ready-to-munch treats. But if you'd prefer to pick up a container especially for the giving of this gift, you certainly have a variety of choices.

Adopt-an-Heirloom

First, and dearest to my heart, is this time-tested approach: in looking for one-of-a-kind containers, indulge in the fun of prowling around flea markets, country fairs, and antique stores. Scour garage sales, estate auctions, Grandma's attic—anywhere there might be vessels that pack along a mystical bit of history all their own. These places yield unique, fascinating, and useful pieces, ranging from crocks, jars, and bottles to hatboxes, cooking pots, tool carriers, and baskets, frequently for a song. Don't ignore the larger containers; you can take some colorful tissue or other paper and line them to provide cushioning and quickly have a great way to present several food gifts together. (See Part III, "Package Deals.")

Old and charming containers can make perfect, endlessly reusable gift items when paired with your handmade food. Consider giving pâté or hummus packed into an antique mold or presenting Irish cream in an antique cream bottle. Once you start browsing, you'll find many possibilities.

Keep in mind that these unique containers will really delight the recipient if once emptied of their tasty contents they can become pretty vases, the perfect storage for precious mementos, or just the right way to present a dried-flower centerpiece.

Spanking New

Of course, new things make nice gifts, too. Today's department stores, malls, hobby shops, and hardware stores have many beautiful jars, bottles, crocks, tins, boxes, baskets, and other vessels. For a few specific suggestions, check "Sources" (Part V).

Those brightly colored little cardboard boxes with the wire handles, clones of the classic Chinese carryout container, are great food holders (line them with paper or cellophane, and only pack them with dry foods, please), and they also take well to decorating with paint or stickers or other decorations. Also useful are coffee-bean bags, which some grocery stores and cafés will part with for pennies.

Baskets

Baskets are often the carrier of choice for gift foods, mostly because of their practicality and ease of use as well as their nostalgic charm. They come in a variety of shapes, sizes, and colors. They summon pictures of European markets, country picnics, and big old-fashioned kitchens. Gift foods have a similar practical but pretty style, so baskets work particularly well for carrying them.

A basket full of food can be presented open to the weather, with just a ribbon or other trimming tied to the handle or woven through the sides and up the top. You can bundle the whole package up in a couple of large pieces of tulle in the same or different colors or use some cellophane, like the gourmet gift shops do. Then I recommend tying the whole thing with a big cheerful bow.

Many of the thematic presents listed in "Package Deals" (Part III) work especially well in baskets. For places to purchase baskets or resources for making your own, see "Sources" (Part V).

Pretty Crafty

To make your gift 100 percent homemade, you can fashion the container yourself. The package becomes another cherished piece of this wonderful homemade gift you've put together.

There are assorted ways to make your own package from scratch. Wooden carriers, boxes, and crates also are something you can craft by hand, often with few tools and little woodworking experience. Lumber supply houses, hobby shops, and craft stores should be able to furnish you with supplies and instructions for this type of project. This sort of carrier is especially nice for a gift, because it can be customized readily with the person's name, a hand-painted design, or some other personal touch.

You might also find lots of unexpected possibilities at craft stores. Fascinating centers for the handy, many of these places yield an abundance of container ideas, from ready-to-decorate Lucite or colored plastic boxes, to unadorned tins and band boxes, to plain canvas bags that are ready for paint or stitchery, to large selections of baskets and unfinished wooden carriers.

Decorations

Designs and Stencils

Painted designs, stencils, and stains are other ways to put the stamp of distinction on gift baskets and boxes or on labels you can later stick on to a jar. Cut out shapes—stars or hearts or abstract polygons—and affix them to a glass jar, using double-stick tape. Then spray paint the jar and let it dry. When you remove the shapes, you'll have a peek-a-boo jar, festive enough to give with pride.

Or you might opt to do the Girl Scout thing to a container, by gluing on items like buttons, trims, seashells, yarn, or whatever embellishments you choose, to help dress it up a bit.

The scrap bag up in the sewing corner also might yield some potential as a resource for home-crafted gift containers. You can use pieces of gingham, calico, felt, or whatever's on hand to cover boxes. A little polyester batting stuffed between the fabric and the box makes a slightly puffy, polished-looking container, and plain drawstring-topped bags of all sizes can be stitched up quickly from bits of fabric. You don't really even have to sew—just cut out squares of material, using pinking shears to create a zig-zag edge, and bundle them around the food, tying the package shut with some string, yarn, or a ribbon. This idea is especially good for dressing up the seasoning packets that go into some of the mixes in chapter 7. You also can use pinked-edge strips of fabric to tie bundles of pasta together for giving.

Rubber Stamps

The rubber stamp market has exploded in recent years, filling gift, stationery, art, and office supply stores with an abundance of stamps in different sizes and designs. There are Victorian flower baskets, fifties-style kitchen gadgets, little animals, whimsical cupids, clever sayings, and many other varieties, all carefully depicted in rubber for your stamping fun. Sold alongside them are ink pads in every color imaginable, including metallic and neon colors.

Stamps are wonderful for decorating your tags and labels, paper bags, cardboard containers, the outer wrapping paper, even on light-colored paper ribbon—whatever part of the package you like. Keep in mind that a single stamp needn't stand alone. Why not make a row of stamps, alternating a flower stamp in one color with a star in another color, or create some other pretty pattern? On tags and labels they work especially well as borders around the name of your gift food.

Just for Appearances

Rare is the package that can't be enhanced with a bit of gratuitous trimming. So, just for appearances and for a change of pace from conventional ribbons and bows, you might want to tie bits of cloth, tulle, raffia, dried grasses, or strips of corn husk onto the necks of bottles or use them to string on the tags. Nature again yields possibilities for this: dried weeds and pinecones always make nice decorations. The container also can be adorned with fresh, dried, or silk flowers or bundles of dried herbs.

Whimsy can be a fun byword in finishing off gifts of food. And here the pack rat reigns: consider using odds and ends squirreled away for the eventual day they'll surely be needed, like colored paper clips (try arranging them mosaic-style); old greeting cards; pretty pictures from past wall calendars; bits of lace; feathers; cut-out words from bright magazines, fashioned into fanciful labels; photos that didn't quite make the family album. All of these things, plus new items like stickers, those collapsible honeycomb holiday decorations sold in stationery stores, streamers, doilies, and miniature toys can be used to give a finishing touch to a food gift.

Another way to adorn bottles of liqueur, juice, vinegar, or flavored oil is to melt some sealing wax and encase the opening of the bottle and cork in it. This makes for an elegant, singular presentation.

It's a Wrap

Wrapping paper is another item you can make yourself. Plain tissue paper, newsprint, pretty pages from magazines (especially those glossy cooking and home decorating publications), shelf lining, and brown Kraft paper are among the less extravagant wrapping materials that can be customized by your own artistic touch. You can, of course, go with fancier papers, such as the sort sold by the sheet in stationery stores, if your gift budget allows it. Try affixing foil stars or other kinds of stickers to the paper, or give it a wash with watercolors. Sponge-painted designs, glitter, and spatter paints are other decorating techniques. Consider the range of media available to you: chalk, acrylic and poster paints, crayons, and markers are just a few.

One fun way to bind up some shapes, like dry mixes, is to roll them up in tissue paper and tie a ribbon around both ends, firecracker-style. Decorating the paper with something sparkly first gives it a particularly festive look. You can put the mix in a plastic bag to start and cover that packaging with the prettier version.

If you opt for pretty ribbons or gilt cords to put the final polish on your present—they're popular gift wrappings for a reason, after all—you might want to bypass the gift wrappings display in the supermarket to seek out more unusual varieties in outlets like florist shops, stationery stores, craft supply places, or sewing centers.

The Basic Bow

No self-respecting giver of gifts can last long without knowing how to tie a decent bow. So here, step by step, is the route to the basic bow:

1. Measure off (but don't cut) enough ribbon to make one loop and one tail of the bow you want. Crimp the ribbon there, and hold the crimp on the package right where you want the bow to be.

2. Pick up the package and slide the spool of ribbon under it, bringing it back up to the top where you're holding the crimped portion. Twist the two pieces to form a cross with the center at the place where you want the bow to be. Check the back side of the package to be sure there are no unsightly twists. Pull the ribbon tight.

3. Measure off the spool-end to be even with the other end, and cut the ribbon from the spool.

4. Slide the just-cut end under the cross's center and tie a knot (this eliminates the need for someone to hold a finger on the center spot).

5. Make a loop with one end, making sure the prettiest side of the ribbon is facing out on both the loop and the tail.

6. Bring the other end up and around the first loop, then loosely draw it through to form the second loop (twist this end as you wrap it over the first loop if you need to keep a pretty side of the ribbon facing out). Adjust the bow, as necessary, so that the loops and ends are even and the pretty side is showing, then carefully pull tight the loops where they lead into the knot.

7. Show all your friends!

There are other, fancier approaches to bow tying. Assorted books have been written on the subject, and if you're interested in honing your ribbon-handling capabilities, I highly recommend seeking out a volume devoted to the subject from your local bookstore or library.

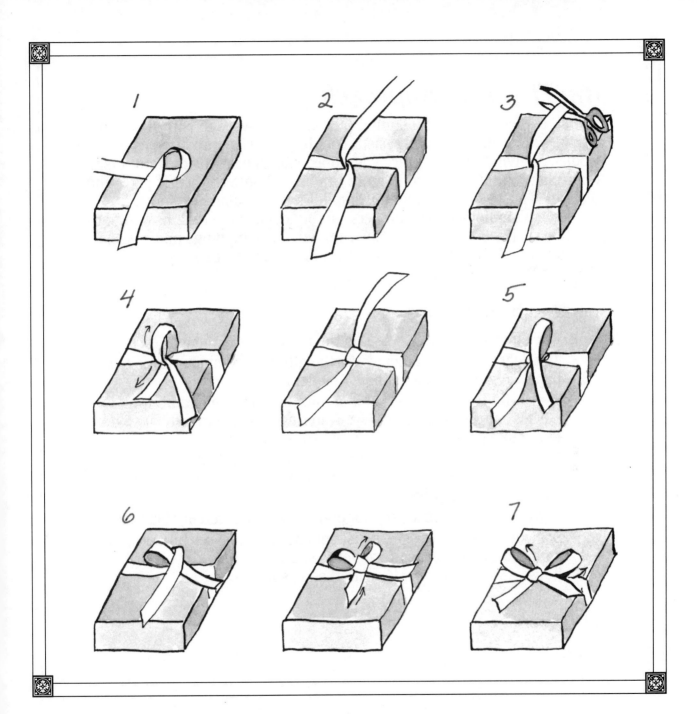

The Thematic Approach

Of course, there are also functional (but still fun) ways to embellish gift packages. You might try tying pasta-cooking utensils onto bundles of noodles or giving nuts in a nicely wrapped package set inside a nut dish. A porcelain-handled spreading knife can be tied onto a crock of pâté, and salad tools make nice accompaniments for gifts of salad dressings.

Some wrappings and containers can befit specific occasions and people. Here's a list of some of my favorite thematic wrappings and vessels. No doubt you'll come up with others, and for more on theme gifts, see "Package Deals" (Part III).

For specific occasions

- For a bon voyage gift, wrap up the food in a road map.
- To celebrate a new career, cover the gift with computer print-out paper or stash it inside a new Rolodex.
- A new-house present might look nice bundled up in a no-longer-needed blueprint, a flower pot, watering can, or virtually any container likely to be useful to the new homeowner.
- For the student going off to college, use the student's old pages of high school homework, a mug, backpack or book bag, a plastic crate, or a laundry basket.
- Consider swaddling a baby food gift in a nice receiving blanket.
- Someone whose house has just sold might like a celebratory gift wrapped in the real estate advertisement that featured his or her house—with a big "sold" written across it by you.

For the individual

- Sheet music makes good wrapping paper for someone who's musically inclined.
- Likewise, pages from old theater programs are appropriate gift wrap for an actor, set designer, or other theater lover.
- Give an investor something delicious wrapped in the stock report pages from the newspaper.
- Goodies for a teacher can be bound in ruled pages from composition books, with the greeting penciled in neatly.
- A cook will be forever grateful for a tasty collection of condiments, pastas, or mixes presented in a handsome copper saucepan, perhaps bound in a cloud of tulle.
- Pages from seed or gardening catalogs, a flower pot, or pretty watering can are nice for a gardener.

Tags and Labels

When it's time to bind it all together and put a tag on the gift, your options again include a wide range of materials. Tags and labels can be fashioned from office supply staples like shipping labels and key tags, decorated with designs of your making, or they can be made from small pieces of high-quality paper cut into interesting shapes. You also can make tags from things found in nature, like unusual twigs (you can fly the tag from it like a little flag), or pieces of thin bark, on which you can write your to/from message.

Tags also can be made using photographs, homemade drawings, even pieces of poetry. A favorite picture, bound in a fabric-covered cardboard frame, makes a very special gift tag with the message written on its back. Or you might fashion a tag by tracing around a cookie cutter onto a piece of cardboard or heavy paper.

Your Own Logo

To personalize your gift further still, you might choose to create a logo, sort of a trademark that always appears on the foods you give. When businesses design logos (or "corporate identities"), they usually begin with the image they want to put forth. You should do the same. Do you want your logo to include words or just a design? If you're using words, such as Gwen's Herb Dressing, ask yourself what visual images seem to go with those words. Perhaps you'll want to write *Herb* in forest green with a leafy flourish.

Make a list of adjectives. Do you want your packages and hence your logo to look sophisticated, spare, folksy, warm, old-fashioned, slick, colorful, muted, funny? Once you have the adjectives, you can associate them with styles and materials. Script calligraphy or stencils will tend to give you an old-fashioned look, which you can then pair with mason jars and gingham, for instance.

Choose from the many decorating techniques available to fashion your own design. Again, rubber stamps, sponge painting, carved linoleum block printing, or stenciling will serve you well. If you're feeling less inspired than that, maybe some graphics from art-oriented computer software would serve your purpose.

If you're planning to give homemade foods on a regular basis, you might find it worthwhile to give a unique look, or even a special name, to your gift-giving enterprise: Edie's Edibles, Doris's Delectables, Ed's Special Sauce, Heavenly Munchies, or simply, "A Gift for You [or recipient's name] from the Kitchen of Mary Jones." Have fun thinking of a name that reflects you and the mood you want your gift foods to inspire.

High Tech

If you happen to have a computer, including the software to produce impressive graphics, you can use it to label your gifts and create your logo. You can use colored paper and script type, a creamy sheet with block letters, funny icons, and graphic design elements. Your options are almost limitless.

Indeed, it would be easy to get lost in the possibilities of presentation. But to get you started, we'll move on to the presents, the recipes themselves. After all, gifts from your kitchen begin with the food.

Present-ation at a Glance

Containers
bags
band boxes
baskets
bottles
canvas bags
cardboard boxes (decorated)
cardboard drums (oatmeal
   containers)
Chinese carryout containers
cooking pots
covered plastic tubs
crates
crocks
hatboxes

jars
molds
tins
wooden carriers

Wrappings
baby blankets
blueprints
cellophane
computer print-out paper
fabric scraps
Kraft paper
lined composition paper
maps
newspaper (especially pertinent
   pages)

newsprint
sheet music
shelf paper
tissue paper
tulle

Decorations
beans
buttons
chalk
colored paper clips
crayons
doilies
dried herbs
embroidery
fabric scraps
feathers
flowers (fresh, dried, or silk)
foil stars
glitter
lace
markers
miniatures
painted designs
paper shapes

pinecones (spray-painted or plain)
rubber stamps
seashells
spatter painting
sponge painting
spray painting
stains
stencils
stickers
streamers
trims
watercolors
weeds (dried)
yarn

Bindings
cloth strips
colored string
corn husks
dried grasses
fabric strips
raffia
ribbons
tulle
yarn

Tags & Labels
bark
computer graphics
cookie-cutter tracings
drawings
framed photographs
key tags
linoleum block printing
magazine cutouts
old greeting card fronts
rubber stamps
shipping labels
twigs

PART II

THE PRESENTS

ONE ▪ *Crowning Glories*

The way we embellish our foods can bring them across the line from the mundane to the marvelous, the mediocre to the magnificent. When you give this transformation as a present, you are helping someone make nice food into wonderful food. Grilled turkey breast is tasty, but grilled turkey breast topped with a dollop of Red Raspberry Chutney is sublime. A dish of homemade vanilla ice cream certainly is a treat, but allow somebody to top it with Maple-Walnut Sauce, and you've given them a lush and comforting dessert that will be long remembered.

You can show your appreciation for these kinds of finishing touches by putting together and giving a condiment or a sauce to help elevate otherwise perfectly acceptable plain foods to just plain perfect. Packaged in attractive crocks or jars, these things constitute the ultimate gesture of impeccable taste.

Salsas: Borrowed Treasure

The Spanish-born sauces that we gringos have lifted so handily for our own adaptations are versatile mixtures, packed with flavor potential. They make great finishing touches when spooned over foods, but they also mix into casseroles and soups in zesty fashion—and, of course, they're terrific as dips.

Green Chile Salsa

Truly an all-purpose condiment, Mexican-style salsa has supplanted even catsup as our favorite topping for everything from eggs to salads to traditional south-of-the-border fare. And when it's homemade, it makes a great gift. This cooked version has a pleasant zip, keeps well, and its heat level can be adjusted to suit the tastes of your recipient.

About 3 cups

1 medium-sized onion, chopped
2 cloves garlic, minced
1 tablespoon olive oil
1 16-ounce can tomatoes, with their juice, mashed by hand
1 4-ounce can chopped green chiles
1 medium-sized bell pepper, diced
1 or 2 fresh jalapeño peppers, seeded and finely chopped
2 teaspoons chili powder
1 teaspoon cumin
Salt and freshly ground pepper to taste
2 tablespoons chopped cilantro

Sauté the onion and garlic gently in the oil until tender. Add the tomatoes, chiles, bell pepper, jalapeños, chili powder, cumin, salt, and pepper. Simmer 30 minutes. Stir in the cilantro; cool. Store tightly covered in the refrigerator.

Apple-Onion Salsa

Perfect with roast pork, this mixture brings flavors sweet and savory into a happy marriage. It's something you can't find in a store and thus makes a great gift.

About 1½ cups

2	tablespoons butter
1	medium-sized onion, finely chopped
1	large, tart apple, peeled, cored, and finely chopped
1	small rib celery, finely chopped
¼	red bell pepper, finely chopped
1	teaspoon chopped fresh thyme or ½ teaspoon dried
1	tablespoon cider vinegar
2	tablespoons white vermouth
1	tablespoon brown sugar

Salt and freshly ground pepper to taste

In a medium saucepan, sauté the onion in the butter just until softened. Stir in the apple, celery, and red pepper and cook, stirring often, until golden. Add the remaining ingredients, stir well, and cook gently for 5 minutes to blend the flavors. Store in the refrigerator. Serve warm or at room temperature.

Sun-Dried Tomato Salsa Italia

This is wonderful as a spread on good crusty bread, but it also serves as a tasty accompaniment to meats, grilled fish, and pasta—any of which would make a nice companion gift.

About ³/₄ cup

¼ cup oil-packed sun-dried tomatoes
1 tablespoon olive oil
¼ cup chopped onion
2 cloves garlic, minced
½ cup freshly grated Romano cheese
2 tablespoons chopped fresh basil
Salt and freshly ground pepper to taste

Drain the tomatoes and chop them up finely. Set aside. Heat the olive oil in a small skillet, and sauté the onion and garlic just until softened. Remove from the heat, and stir in the tomatoes. Mix well. Fold in the cheese and basil; season to taste. Store tightly covered in the refrigerator. Serve at room temperature.

Pineapple Salsa

A delectable union of sweet and spice, this mixture is delicious with chicken enchiladas, grilled fish, or pork. If you like to fish, you can heroically present a jar of this, along with the day's catch, to a deserving friend. Keeps about 5 days.

About 1⅓ cups

1	cup finely chopped fresh pineapple
¼	cup sliced scallions
1	to 2 fresh jalapeño peppers, seeded and minced
2	tablespoons chopped cilantro
1	teaspoon fresh lime juice
Pinch of salt	

Mix all the ingredients together gently. Cover and chill. Serve at room temperature.

Fajita Kit

Consider stocking a good, sturdy basket with a jar of Pineapple Salsa and some good, freshly made tortillas, a couple of plump chicken breasts, maybe a sweet onion and a bright red bell pepper from the local farm stand, and either a sack of exotic grilling charcoal or a nice hefty fajita pan—depending on your recipient's current climate. It's a ready-to-cook fajita feast.

Pesto: Haste to the Paste

The traditional Italian basil-based seasoning paste has opened new culinary doors in America and elsewhere, whether tucked into a batch of scrambled eggs, tossed with a plate of freshly cooked linguine, spread over a slab of ripe tomato, or tucked into a pot of savory tomato sauce. But there are lots of ways to extend the idea of pesto to other featured flavors and to bend the parameters of pesto's uses. The concept—and the flavors that result from its expansion—bear sharing with those deserving of your gift-giving talents.

Powerful Pesto

As part of a clustering of gifts, few items are more dynamic than flavorful Basil Pesto. It's good to include with any gift of pasta or as a companion to Marinara or Alfredo Sauce. Given with a basket of ruby-red, vine-fresh tomatoes from your garden, it's a celebration of summer flavors. Include with those things a few slices of provolone cheese and a good loaf of bread, and it's a lunch kit: slabs of homegrown tomatoes slathered with pesto, teamed up with a smooth cheese, and hugged between two slices of bread make one of summer's finest possible lunch offerings.

Other additions could be a bottle of wine, a Pavarotti tape, red-checkered tablecloth, whatever strikes your fancy.

Fresh Basil Pesto

Infinitely, deliciously adaptable, the savory Italian herb paste that is classic pesto is a good thing to give fresh in large quantities or frozen in not-so-large portions (an ice cube tray works well for making flavorful nugget-sized portions), to use whenever the mood strikes. If there's a stash of pesto in the freezer, the mood will strike often. And you'll be remembered fondly every time the frozen treasure is tapped.

About 2 cups

2	cups packed fresh basil leaves
3	cloves garlic, finely chopped
½	cup pine nuts
¼	cup chopped pecans
1	cup freshly grated imported Parmesan cheese
⅓	cup olive oil (or more, if desired)

Salt and freshly ground pepper to taste

Unless you have a large mortar and pestle on hand—and are comfortably adept at using it—you'll need a good blender or a food processor to make this. Chop the basil by pulsing the motor for a couple of seconds at a time, scraping the blender jar or work bowl as needed, until evenly chopped. Add the garlic and nuts and continue to chop, stopping to scrape the bowl once or twice, until well mixed.

Sprinkle the cheese over the pesto and pulse it in, then turn the motor on and dribble the oil through the open jar or the feed tube, turning the motor off as soon as the oil is all added. Transfer the pesto to another container, season as desired, and store, tightly covered, in the refrigerator for up to 6 weeks or so, or in the freezer for as long as a year.

Note: If you plan to give the pesto frozen, be prepared to keep it well chilled while it's being transported; otherwise the cubes will melt.

Black Bean Pesto

This fat-free mixture is good as a dip for tortilla chips but serves equally well as a garnish for grilled chicken or fish, rice, or pasta, and it's a natural with Green Chile Salsa (see Index), given along with a bag of good tortilla chips. You also might suggest trying it in a fajita.

About 2 cups

1	15-ounce can black beans, drained
1	clove garlic, minced
¼	cup finely chopped onion
½	medium-sized yellow pepper, chopped into ¼-inch dice
1	medium-sized jalapeño pepper, cored, seeded, and minced
½	cup beer
½	teaspoon salt
	Freshly ground pepper to taste
¼	teaspoon cumin
⅛	teaspoon cayenne pepper
2	tablespoons chopped cilantro

Combine the beans, garlic, onion, bell pepper, jalapeño, and beer in a medium saucepan. Bring to a boil; reduce the heat to medium and let it bubble gently, stirring often, for 20 to 30 minutes, until the liquid is mostly gone and the beans are tender. Stir in the remaining ingredients, and mash with a potato masher or in a food processor until the mixture has a chunky-paste consistency. Store the pesto, covered, in the refrigerator. Serve warm or at room temperature.

Sage Pesto

The assertive character of fresh sage distinguishes this pesto, which is delicious with pasta, chicken, or fish or used in a dip or spread for appetizers. Giving it as a gift is a good way to share with others the bounty of a healthy sage plant in your garden.

About 2 cups

⅓   **cup hazelnuts**
3   **large cloves garlic**
2   **cups fresh sage leaves (loosely packed)**
⅔   **cup olive oil**
1   **cup freshly grated Parmesan cheese (grate it fine)**
Salt and freshly ground pepper to taste

Preheat the oven to 350 degrees. Spread out the hazelnuts on a baking sheet and toast them for about 10 minutes, until they are lightly browned and the skins are papery. Take from the oven, cool slightly, and rub off the skins.

Turn the food processor on and drop the garlic cloves, one by one, through the feed chute. Chop them well, scraping down the sides once, then put the nuts in and process in 2-second pulses until well chopped. Add the sage and oil and process until uniform, but don't puree. Sprinkle on the cheese and pulse it in. Season the pesto as desired.

Transfer the mixture to one or more containers; cover and chill or freeze until ready to use. Serve at room temperature.

Eggplant Pesto

Spooned onto roast or grilled lamb, this evokes memories of moussaka, so it makes a good thing to give to the lamb lovers who travel in your circle. But it also is good with other meats or tossed with hot pasta or freshly cooked rice.

About 3 cups

1	medium-sized eggplant
3	tablespoons olive oil
1	medium-sized onion, chopped
2	cloves garlic, minced
1	large tomato, peeled, seeded, and finely diced
½	cup minced walnuts
2	teaspoons chopped fresh dill weed
1	teaspoon chopped fresh rosemary
⅓	cup freshly grated imported Parmesan cheese

Peel the eggplant, and cut it into ¼-inch dice. Put it in a colander, salt it lightly, and set it over a drainboard for 20 to 30 minutes.

Heat the olive oil in a large skillet. Working with a handful at a time, squeeze out the excess moisture from the eggplant, and put it in the skillet along with the onion and garlic. Sauté the mixture over medium heat, stirring often, until very tender, about 10 minutes. Stir in the tomato, nuts, and herbs. Cook over medium-low heat for another 5 minutes. Remove from the stove and cool. Stir in the cheese and chill. Serve warm or at room temperature.

Chutney: Sweet and Sour Heaven

No longer the exclusive condiment of the Indian peninsula, chutney has found its way to our hearts and palates through its sheer dynamic deliciousness. We use chutney to top off meats, in salad dressings, or even dumped over cream cheese or Brie as a spreadable treat with breads and crackers. Or, for a more traditional way to enjoy chutney, try it as part of the condiment buffet with a curry dish or tossed with freshly cooked rice, as they do in India.

Tomato-Apple Chutney

Traditional home-canned chutney, brimming with freshly picked apples and tomatoes, is a perennially favorite way for cooks to celebrate the fall yield—and to share its joys with those they love.

6 to 7 half-pints

>9–10 medium-sized ripe tomatoes
>6–7 medium-sized tart apples
>½ cup chopped green pepper
>1½ cups chopped onion
>1 cup raisins
>2 teaspoons salt
>2 cups cider vinegar
>2 tablespoons pickling spice

In a large, nonaluminum kettle or saucepan, stir together the tomatoes, apples, green pepper, onion, raisins, salt, and vinegar. Tie the pickling spice up in a square of cheesecloth and add it to the pan. Bring the mixture to a simmer, and cook 1 hour, stirring often, until thickened. Transfer to storage containers and chill, or put into hot, sterilized half-pint jars and seal according to the instructions in Part IV ("Basics"), processing the jars for 5 minutes.

Red Raspberry Chutney

Delicious on roast or grilled poultry, this sweet/sour specialty has a gorgeous deep-red color. Take some to your next chicken cookout.

About 6 half-pints

4	cups raspberries (fresh or frozen, unsweetened)
4	cups cored, peeled, chopped tart apples
4	cloves garlic, minced
3	tablespoons chopped fresh ginger
1	tablespoon dry mustard
1	tablespoon salt

Pinch of cayenne pepper
1½ cups cider vinegar

1	cup packed brown sugar
2	cups raisins

Combine the raspberries, apples, garlic, ginger, mustard, salt, and cayenne pepper in a nonaluminum kettle. Mix well, then stir in the vinegar. Simmer until the berries are soft, about 5 minutes. Add the sugar and raisins, and cook, stirring occasionally, for 45 to 55 minutes, or until thick. Transfer to covered containers and chill, or put into hot, sterilized half-pint jars and seal, following the instructions in Part IV ("Basics"), processing the jars for 10 minutes.

Pear Chutney

The mellow sweetness of pears is perfectly suited for chutney. This mixture tastes delicious with roast pork, though it also works with salads or curries. It's a one-of-a-kind gift item.

6 half-pints

> 5 cups peeled, seeded, chopped pears (5 or 6 medium-sized)
> 1 lemon, seeds removed, finely chopped (including skin)
> 1 clove garlic, minced
> 2 cups firmly packed brown sugar
> 1½ cups raisins
> 2 tablespoons minced fresh ginger
> ½ of a vanilla bean, split lengthwise
> 1½ teaspoons salt
> Pinch of cayenne pepper
> 1½ cups cider vinegar

Combine all the ingredients and cook gently in a large, nonaluminum saucepan, stirring often, until the fruit is tender and the mixture has thickened slightly, about 60 to 75 minutes. Remove the vanilla bean. Ladle the chutney into covered containers, or put into hot, sterilized half-pint jars and seal according to the directions in Part IV ("Basics"), processing the jars for 10 minutes.

Concord Grape Chutney

An autumn delight, this rich mixture is wonderful with pork or roasted poultry. If you seal it in a boiling water bath, you'll have it on hand to give at holiday time.

6 to 7 half-pints

6   cups Concord grapes
2   large apples (any kind except Red Delicious), peeled, cored, and chopped
1   medium-sized onion, chopped
2   cloves garlic, finely chopped
1   cup chopped sweetened dried pineapple
2   teaspoons mustard seed
½   teaspoon ginger
Pinch of cayenne pepper
1½ cups cider vinegar
½   cup honey
1½ cups dried currants
1   piece of lemon peel (yellow part only), about 1 inch wide and 4 inches long

Slip the skins off the grapes, dropping the skins into a large kettle and putting the pulp into a medium saucepan. Bring the pulp to a boil; put it through a food mill or strainer to remove the seeds. Put the strained pulp into the kettle along with all the remaining ingredients. Cook at a gentle bubble, partially covered, stirring occasionally, until thick, about 40 to 50 minutes. Store in covered containers in the refrigerator or put into hot, sterilized half-pint jars, cover, and seal according to the directions in Part IV ("Basics"), processing the jars for 10 minutes.

Relish: Home-Turf Counterpart

Though we Americans only now are beginning to explore the potential of chutney, we've had our own answer to the Indian condiment for some time, in the mixtures of finely chopped vegetables, sugar, and vinegar that we call relish. They're perfect foils for meats of all kinds, and they're easy to make.

Red Pepper Relish

A simple, colorful, and savory accompaniment for almost any kind of meat, or you can suggest it as a garnish for pasta dishes. It contrasts beautifully with basil pesto, so you might give it with some of that, too. It also is delicious eaten with mozzarella cheese (a good companion gift) or slathered onto crusty bread (another good thing to tuck into the basket). It can be used as a sandwich condiment, along with standard cold cuts, or with egg salad—a true taste sensation, and an important component of any self-respecting picnic basket.

About 1½ cups

1 large red bell pepper
2 tablespoons olive oil
½ cup finely chopped onion
2 cloves garlic, minced
Salt and freshly ground pepper to taste
1–2 tablespoons balsamic vinegar

Place the red pepper under the broiler and roast it, turning to expose all sides to the heat, until it is uniformly charred. Take it out, drop it in a brown paper bag, crimp the top shut, and let the pepper cool in the bag for about 10 minutes. Then pull off all the skin and remove the core, ribs, and seeds. Chop the pepper quite fine and set aside.

Heat the olive oil in a medium skillet, and sauté the onion and garlic over medium heat until translucent. Stir in the red pepper and season to taste. Remove from the heat; dribble in a few drops of vinegar and mix well. Taste and add more vinegar, if desired.

Store the relish in the refrigerator in a covered container. Serve warm or at room temperature.

Confetti Relish

Full of color and fresh flavors, this "raw" condiment goes well on meats, or it can be used to liven up a quesadilla or to top off manicotti or cannelloni. And its colors make it a handsome thing to give away.

About 2 cups

½ cup oil-packed sun-dried tomatoes, drained and minced
½ cup each: green, yellow, and purple bell peppers, cored, seeded, and minced
2 scallions, minced (include some green part)
1 medium-sized clove garlic, minced
½ teaspoon thyme
Salt and freshly ground pepper to taste
1 tablespoon balsamic vinegar
1 teaspoon olive oil

   Toss the tomatoes, peppers, scallions, and garlic together, mixing well. Add the thyme, salt, and pepper, and toss again. Drizzle on the vinegar and oil, and toss once more. Store, tightly covered, in the refrigerator. Serve at room temperature.

Cranberry-Maple Relish

Luscious and amazingly easy to put together, this possibly could help stamp out can-shaped cranberry sauces. If you're invited to Thanksgiving dinner, volunteer to bring the cranberry sauce. Your hosts will be delighted when you turn up with this instead. Don't save it strictly for the holiday table, though; it's also wonderful with roast chicken and game.

About 1¹/₂ cups

2	cups cranberries
²/₃	cup pure maple syrup
¼	cup chopped pecans
1	teaspoon grated orange rind
1	tablespoon balsamic vinegar

Combine the berries and syrup in a medium saucepan, and bring to a boil. Let them bubble gently, stirring often, until the skins on the cranberries have all split and the mixture has thickened, 2 to 3 minutes. If some of the berries don't burst, press them gently against the side of the pan with the back of your spoon to pop them, being careful to avoid hot splatters.

While the berries are cooking, put the pecans in a small, dry skillet, and stir them over medium heat until they are fragrant and lightly toasted. Transfer to a plate to cool.

When the cranberry mixture has thickened, take it off the heat and stir in the orange rind, vinegar, and pecans. Mix well. Transfer to a covered container and chill.

Sauces: Partners in Perfection

Whether tossed in, slathered over, or served plateside for dipping, a sauce can bring new depth and excitement to a meal. The distinctive seasonings and textures added by a well-chosen sauce sometimes mean the difference between good food and great food. No wonder a jar of one of these mixtures makes such a terrific gift, particularly when it's accompanied by one of the foods with which it is so tasty.

Maple Mustard Sauce

This dipping sauce couldn't be simpler. It's the perfect companion gift to a good smoked ham.

Use equal parts:
Dijon mustard
Pure maple syrup

Mix the mustard and syrup. Store, tightly covered, in the refrigerator.

Alfredo Sauce

Rich and sumptuous, this rendition of the versatile Roman sauce that goes by the name Alfredo transforms a plate of lonely pasta into a feast. It's an especially nice thing to give to someone who has visited Rome and remembers fondly savoring the original version at Alfredo's.

About 1¼ cups

> 2 tablespoons butter
> 2 tablespoons minced onion
> 2 tablespoons flour
> 1 cup milk
> Salt and freshly ground pepper to taste
> ½ teaspoon dry mustard
> A few grains cayenne pepper
> ½ cup freshly grated imported Parmesan cheese

Melt the butter in a small saucepan, and sauté the onion over medium-low heat until it is translucent, about 10 minutes, stirring often. Increase the heat to medium, stir in the flour, and cook the roux, stirring constantly, for about 2 minutes. Pour in the milk, and stir briskly until smooth. Add the seasonings and continue cooking, stirring constantly, until the sauce is thickened. Remove from the heat, mix in the cheese, and stir until it melts. Transfer the sauce to an attractive vessel, cover it tightly, and store it in the refrigerator. When you present it, be sure to advise that, at serving time, the sauce must be reheated very gently to prevent curdling.

Marinara Sauce

Classic homemade red pasta sauce can be as easy to use as opening a jar—once you've done the preliminary work. A welcome, labor-free gift.

About 4 cups

3	tablespoons olive oil
1	medium-sized onion, chopped
¼	cup dry white wine
2	16-ounce cans unsalted tomatoes with juice, pureed
1	6-ounce can tomato paste
2	cloves garlic, finely chopped
¼	cup chopped fresh parsley
1	teaspoon dried basil
1	teaspoon dried oregano
½	teaspoon dried thyme
¼	teaspoon dried marjoram
1	teaspoon sugar

A few grains cayenne pepper
Salt and freshly ground pepper to taste

Heat the oil in a large saucepan, and sauté the onion until softened. Add the wine, and cook over medium heat until the liquid has almost all evaporated, 10 to 15 minutes. Stir in the remaining ingredients and mix well. Cook gently, stirring often, for about an hour. Cover the pan partially if the sauce sputters too much.

Ladle the sauce into 1- to 2-cup containers. Cover tightly and refrigerate or freeze until ready to use.

Relish: Home-Turf Counterpart

Though we Americans only now are beginning to explore the potential of chutney, we've had our own answer to the Indian condiment for some time, in the mixtures of finely chopped vegetables, sugar, and vinegar that we call relish. They're perfect foils for meats of all kinds, and they're easy to make.

Red Pepper Relish

A simple, colorful, and savory accompaniment for almost any kind of meat, or you can suggest it as a garnish for pasta dishes. It contrasts beautifully with basil pesto, so you might give it with some of that, too. It also is delicious eaten with mozzarella cheese (a good companion gift) or slathered onto crusty bread (another good thing to tuck into the basket). It can be used as a sandwich condiment, along with standard cold cuts, or with egg salad—a true taste sensation, and an important component of any self-respecting picnic basket.

About 1½ cups

1   large red bell pepper
2   tablespoons olive oil
½   cup finely chopped onion
2   cloves garlic, minced
Salt and freshly ground pepper to taste
1–2 tablespoons balsamic vinegar

Place the red pepper under the broiler and roast it, turning to expose all sides to the heat, until it is uniformly charred. Take it out, drop it in a brown paper bag, crimp the top shut, and let the pepper cool in the bag for about 10 minutes. Then pull off all the skin and remove the core, ribs, and seeds. Chop the pepper quite fine and set aside.

Heat the olive oil in a medium skillet, and sauté the onion and garlic over medium heat until translucent. Stir in the red pepper and season to taste. Remove from the heat; dribble in a few drops of vinegar and mix well. Taste and add more vinegar, if desired.

Store the relish in the refrigerator in a covered container. Serve warm or at room temperature.

Confetti Relish

Full of color and fresh flavors, this "raw" condiment goes well on meats, or it can be used to liven up a quesadilla or to top off manicotti or cannelloni. And its colors make it a handsome thing to give away.

About 2 cups

½ cup oil-packed sun-dried tomatoes, drained and minced
½ cup each: green, yellow, and purple bell peppers, cored, seeded, and minced
2 scallions, minced (include some green part)
1 medium-sized clove garlic, minced
½ teaspoon thyme
Salt and freshly ground pepper to taste
1 tablespoon balsamic vinegar
1 teaspoon olive oil

Toss the tomatoes, peppers, scallions, and garlic together, mixing well. Add the thyme, salt, and pepper, and toss again. Drizzle on the vinegar and oil, and toss once more. Store, tightly covered, in the refrigerator. Serve at room temperature.

Cranberry-Maple Relish

Luscious and amazingly easy to put together, this possibly could help stamp out can-shaped cranberry sauces. If you're invited to Thanksgiving dinner, volunteer to bring the cranberry sauce. Your hosts will be delighted when you turn up with this instead. Don't save it strictly for the holiday table, though; it's also wonderful with roast chicken and game.

About 1¹/₂ cups

2	**cups cranberries**
²/₃	**cup pure maple syrup**
¹/₄	**cup chopped pecans**
1	**teaspoon grated orange rind**
1	**tablespoon balsamic vinegar**

Combine the berries and syrup in a medium saucepan, and bring to a boil. Let them bubble gently, stirring often, until the skins on the cranberries have all split and the mixture has thickened, 2 to 3 minutes. If some of the berries don't burst, press them gently against the side of the pan with the back of your spoon to pop them, being careful to avoid hot splatters.

While the berries are cooking, put the pecans in a small, dry skillet, and stir them over medium heat until they are fragrant and lightly toasted. Transfer to a plate to cool.

When the cranberry mixture has thickened, take it off the heat and stir in the orange rind, vinegar, and pecans. Mix well. Transfer to a covered container and chill.

Sauces: Partners in Perfection

Whether tossed in, slathered over, or served plateside for dipping, a sauce can bring new depth and excitement to a meal. The distinctive seasonings and textures added by a well-chosen sauce sometimes mean the difference between good food and great food. No wonder a jar of one of these mixtures makes such a terrific gift, particularly when it's accompanied by one of the foods with which it is so tasty.

Maple Mustard Sauce

This dipping sauce couldn't be simpler. It's the perfect companion gift to a good smoked ham.

Use equal parts:
   Dijon mustard
   Pure maple syrup

Mix the mustard and syrup. Store, tightly covered, in the refrigerator.

Alfredo Sauce

Rich and sumptuous, this rendition of the versatile Roman sauce that goes by the name Alfredo transforms a plate of lonely pasta into a feast. It's an especially nice thing to give to someone who has visited Rome and remembers fondly savoring the original version at Alfredo's.

About 1¼ cups

> 2   **tablespoons butter**
> 2   **tablespoons minced onion**
> 2   **tablespoons flour**
> 1   **cup milk**
> **Salt and freshly ground pepper to taste**
> ½   **teaspoon dry mustard**
> **A few grains cayenne pepper**
> ½   **cup freshly grated imported Parmesan cheese**

Melt the butter in a small saucepan, and sauté the onion over medium-low heat until it is translucent, about 10 minutes, stirring often. Increase the heat to medium, stir in the flour, and cook the roux, stirring constantly, for about 2 minutes. Pour in the milk, and stir briskly until smooth. Add the seasonings and continue cooking, stirring constantly, until the sauce is thickened. Remove from the heat, mix in the cheese, and stir until it melts. Transfer the sauce to an attractive vessel, cover it tightly, and store it in the refrigerator. When you present it, be sure to advise that, at serving time, the sauce must be reheated very gently to prevent curdling.

Marinara Sauce

Classic homemade red pasta sauce can be as easy to use as opening a jar—once you've done the preliminary work. A welcome, labor-free gift.

About 4 cups

3	tablespoons olive oil
1	medium-sized onion, chopped
¼	cup dry white wine
2	16-ounce cans unsalted tomatoes with juice, pureed
1	6-ounce can tomato paste
2	cloves garlic, finely chopped
¼	cup chopped fresh parsley
1	teaspoon dried basil
1	teaspoon dried oregano
½	teaspoon dried thyme
¼	teaspoon dried marjoram
1	teaspoon sugar
	A few grains cayenne pepper
	Salt and freshly ground pepper to taste

Heat the oil in a large saucepan, and sauté the onion until softened. Add the wine, and cook over medium heat until the liquid has almost all evaporated, 10 to 15 minutes. Stir in the remaining ingredients and mix well. Cook gently, stirring often, for about an hour. Cover the pan partially if the sauce sputters too much.

Ladle the sauce into 1- to 2-cup containers. Cover tightly and refrigerate or freeze until ready to use.

Barbecue Sauce

This all-purpose, indoor-outdoor potion works just as well with baby back ribs slow-roasted in the oven as it does brushed over chicken pieces sizzling on the backyard grill. If you know somebody who pines for outdoor-cooked meals in the dead of winter, this would be a perfect food to give.

About 2¹/₂ cups

> 2   tablespoons butter
> ¾   cup minced onion
> ¾   cup minced celery
> 1   cup catsup
> ½   cup chili sauce
> ½   teaspoon prepared horseradish
> ½   cup water
> 4   teaspoons Worcestershire sauce
> 2   tablespoons vinegar
> 2   tablespoons dark brown sugar
> 2   tablespoons freshly squeezed lemon juice

Melt the butter in a medium saucepan, and sauté the onion and celery until they are tender. Stir in the catsup, chili sauce, horseradish, water, Worcestershire, vinegar, and sugar; mix thoroughly. Bring to a simmer, and cook gently, stirring occasionally, for about 30 minutes. Remove from the heat, stir in the lemon juice, and let cool. Store, covered tightly, in the refrigerator.

If you prefer, put the sauce into hot, sterilized canning jars, top with new lids and rings, and process them for 40 minutes in a boiling-water bath, following the general instructions given in Part IV ("Basics").

TWO · *Take a Dip, Put Out a Spread*

Few things spell cordiality better than first-course foods. When you offer your guests something delicious to nibble on right off the bat, you're sending out the message that you're glad they came, that they matter to you, that making their taste buds happy is important to you.

So it follows that giving one of these things as a present is nothing short of grace in action. They're perfect for bringing along to the party, a way of saying thanks for the hospitality. "Fancy," delicatessen-style dips and spreads come through with ultimate warmth and delectability when they're prepared at home. Ditto for flavored butters, which are wonderful indulgences (and thus great gifts), and specialized mustards. Both are tasty flavor enhancers that can be squirreled away in the refrigerator or freezer, waiting to be called into action to make an everyday food into something extraordinary. To the food lover, such stashes are akin to money in the bank.

Pinto Bean Dip

Zesty and versatile, this mixture is as good rolled up in a tortilla or spooned onto the supper plate for a side dish as it is when used for a dunking substance for crispy chips. Anyone with a taste for Mexican food will appreciate receiving a batch of this flavorful dip.

About 2¹/₂ cups

1	cup dry pinto beans
1	medium-sized onion, chopped
3	cloves garlic, minced
2	or 3 jalapeño peppers, minced
2	teaspoons chili powder
1	teaspoon ground cumin
¼	teaspoon cayenne pepper

Salt to taste

2	tablespoons lard or vegetable oil

Sort through the beans, removing any shriveled ones or dirt clumps. Rinse thoroughly, then cover with cold water and set aside to soak overnight.

Drain off the soaking liquid and place the beans in a large, covered pot with plenty of fresh water. Add the onion, garlic, and jalapeños; bring to a boil. Reduce the heat, partially cover the pan, and let it simmer for several hours, stirring occasionally, until the beans are very tender and the mixture resembles thick bean soup. You might need to replenish the water during cooking, but don't add more than you need or the dip will be too thin.

Mash the beans lightly, mixing in the chili powder, cumin, cayenne, and salt as you go.

Melt the lard in a small pan and when it is very hot, stir it into the beans, mixing only until the fat is absorbed. Store the dip, covered, in the refrigerator. Serve hot or warm.

Red Bean Hummus

The lush Middle Eastern chickpea dip/spread takes a rosy twist with the inclusion of some red beans. This makes a large quantity, but it freezes well. It also halves quite well. When you give it away, a package of pita bread, to be quartered and used for dipping, makes a good companion.

About 6 cups

1	15-ounce can red kidney beans, drained
2	19-ounce cans garbanzo beans, drained
⅔	cup tahini (sesame seed paste)
2	tablespoons freshly squeezed lemon juice
½	cup warm water
⅓	cup olive oil
3	or 4 cloves garlic, minced
1	tablespoon salt
2	teaspoons ground cumin
	Freshly ground pepper to taste

Combine the beans, tahini, lemon juice, water, and oil in a food processor, and process until smooth, stopping once or twice to scrape down the sides of the work bowl. Add the garlic and seasonings, and process to blend. Store in covered containers in the refrigerator or freezer.

Spicy Peanut Dipping Sauce

A cocktail buffet is greatly enhanced with the inclusion of bite-sized bits of grilled chicken or pork to dip into this zesty mixture.

1 1/2 cups

½ cup smooth peanut butter
¾ cup lukewarm chicken stock (preferably homemade)
2 tablespoons minced fresh jalapeño peppers (1–2 medium-sized)
1 tablespoon minced cilantro
1–2 cloves garlic, minced
1 teaspoon sesame oil

Combine the peanut butter and stock in a blender or food processor, and mix until smooth. Add the peppers, cilantro, and garlic; mix until uniform. Scrape down the sides, and add the oil, blending just until it is incorporated. Store, tightly covered, in the refrigerator. Serve at room temperature.

Gramma's Chicken Liver Pâté

Smooth, rich, and perfectly seasoned, Gramma Chickering's tasty rendition of pâté always made "the cocktail hour" something special. She used to pack it into handsome ceramic crocks, from which we would spread it on crackers. It's an elegant thing to give during the holidays and beyond.

About 4 cups

1 cup (2 sticks) butter, divided
1 pound chicken livers, coarsely chopped
4 shallots, finely minced
3 large hard-boiled eggs, chopped
½ teaspoon salt
⅛ teaspoon cloves
¼ teaspoon each: pepper, thyme, marjoram, ground ginger, and ground cinnamon
2 tablespoons Madeira
2 tablespoons brandy

Cook the chicken livers and shallots slowly in one stick of butter, being careful not to brown them. Remove from the heat when the livers are firm but still tender, about 10 to 15 minutes.

In a food processor, cream the remaining stick of butter until smooth. Add the cooked livers and shallots with their juices, the eggs, the seasonings, Madeira, and brandy. Pulse to mix everything well, then scrape down the sides of the work bowl and process until the mixture is pureed. Pack the pate into crocks, cover them, and refrigerate until ready to serve.

"I like very much to make terrines now and then. In small pots they are fine for presents....But for one of the nicest celebrations I ever went to, small and quiet and vitally important, as all such things should be (it was the marriage of my younger daughter), we ate perhaps the simplest pâté ever evolved over several thousand years by a wandering people. It was exactly right: light and fresh. It was made with loving care by an Orthodox Jewish godmother and eaten by an ecumenical crew of Presbyterians, Episcopalians, Orthodox Greeks, Catholics, atheists, and back sliders, with equal pleasure."—from *With Bold Knife & Fork,* by M. F. K. Fisher (Putnam's, 1969)

Do-It-Yourself Boursin

My sister, Joan Marquart, devised this flavorful spread. Its quantity of garlic is variable, but Joan notes, "The more, the better." I tend to agree, but you should use your own tastes—or those of the recipient of your gift—as a guide.

About 2¹/₂ cups

2   8-ounce packages cream cheese, softened
1   8-ounce tub lightly salted whipped butter
1–2 cloves garlic, minced
1   teaspoon oregano
¹/₄ teaspoon each: basil, marjoram, thyme, and freshly ground black pepper

Smash everything together by hand, or use a food processor. Pack into crocks or jars and chill. Also can be frozen.

Nancy's Hot Pepper Jelly

Nancy Frick, my sister-in-law, put this in the family cookbook with this warning: Wear gloves when handling hot peppers! The jelly is good over cream cheese or Brie as a spread for crackers, but Nancy recommends serving it over a flavored cream cheese, such as Do-It-Yourself Boursin (also in this chapter). Consider teaming the two with some crackers for a nice gift. You might mention that this jelly is also good to use in lieu of that pinch of sugar in your favorite chili recipe.

About 5 half-pints

> 1½ cups green bell peppers, seeded, cored, and finely chopped
> ½ cup jalapeño peppers, seeded, cored, and finely chopped
> 1½ cups vinegar
> 6½ cups sugar
> 1 packet Certo pectin
> 2–3 drops green food coloring

Combine the peppers, vinegar, and sugar in a saucepan; heat slowly, stirring often, to a boil. Boil gently for 8 minutes. Remove from the heat and cool 10 minutes. Add the pectin and food coloring. Pour into hot, sterilized jars, and top immediately with one melted bar of paraffin.

Butters

In this age of saturated-fat phobia, butter has donned the flowing black cape of the arch villain. This is a shame, because while few people can wolf down large amounts of fats without a thought to health matters and weight gain, most of us can help ourselves to an occasional pat of butter without fearing too deeply for our lives. At times like those, butters like these make perfect flavor enhancers.

While it's true that margarine is no better in terms of fat content than butter, for those with cholesterol to consider, it usually is the better choice. If the circumstances of your intended recipient call for margarine, be sure to select a high-quality one. And I'll leave it up to you what to call it.

Pasta Butter

This does just what the name implies—it makes noodles into instant dinner—but that's not to say you can't just as well spread it on crusty bread. Its versatility and savory spunk make it a great gift.

One 4-ounce log

½   cup butter, softened
2   tablespoons minced fresh herbs of your choice (basil, oregano, thyme, parsley, and/or marjoram—use at least two)
1   or 2 cloves garlic, minced
3   tablespoons freshly grated Parmesan or Romano cheese
Salt and freshly ground pepper to taste

Cream everything together, and form into a log roughly the size of the butter when it was still a stick. Wrap in wax paper, then plastic wrap or freezer paper, and freeze until firm. Store in the freezer or the refrigerator until needed.

Well-Dressed Butters

The perfect thing to present a flavored butter in is a butter dish, if your gift budget allows it. There is an amazing variety of butter dishes to be found in china shops, antiques stores, and gift stores, from whimsical cow-topped sets to ornate Victorian pieces to sleek and contemporary holders. With your luscious butter inside and a lush bow on top, it makes an elegant and indulgent gift.

Raspberry Butter

A wonderful breakfast treat when slathered on toast, waffles, or an English muffin, this spread makes good use of fresh raspberries that are just a shade too ripe. And its rosiness makes it a beautiful gift to behold, nestled in a basket alongside some good bakery.

One 4-ounce log

½   cup butter, softened
¼   cup fresh or frozen (without syrup, thawed) raspberries, at room temperature
2   tablespoons sifted powdered sugar

Cream the butter, berries, and sugar together until the mixture is evenly pink throughout. Form into a log, about the size of a stick of butter, and wrap in wax paper. Seal with plastic wrap or freezer paper, and freeze until firm. Store in the freezer or refrigerator until ready to use, but soften slightly before serving.

Cilantro-Lime Butter

Perfect with grilled fish, this simple mixture brings out the flavor of foods with its sheer freshness. Offer a batch of this butter with the fish that didn't get away.

One 4-ounce log

½   cup butter, softened
2   tablespoons chopped cilantro
1   tablespoon freshly squeezed lime juice
A few grains cayenne pepper

Combine everything and blend thoroughly. Form into a log, about the size of a stick of butter, and wrap in wax paper. Seal with plastic wrap or freezer paper, and freeze until firm. Store in the refrigerator, or keep frozen until ready to use. Soften slightly, so the butter can be sliced into pats, before serving.

Mustard Butter

This is a good sandwich spread, in addition to being suitable over almost any kind of grilled or broiled meat. Good to include with a collection of picnic foods.

One 4-ounce log

½   cup butter, softened
1   tablespoon Dijon mustard
1   clove garlic, minced
1   tablespoon chopped parsley
Salt and freshly ground pepper to taste

Combine everything and blend well. Form the butter into a log, about the size of a stick of butter, and wrap in wax paper. Freeze until firm. Thaw slightly before using in slices. Store any unused butter in the refrigerator or freezer.

Maître d'Hôtel Butter

A classic spread that works on almost anything, be it animal, vegetable, or—well, I said almost *anything. The amicable flavors of lemon and parsley can be used to bring out the flavors of seafoods, poultry, or red meats, and they also enhance such supporting players as broccoli, green beans, and carrots (so this butter is a nice thing to give along with the delicious things you've grown in your garden).*

Two 4-ounce logs

⅔ cup loosely packed parsley leaves (use the Italian flat-leaf variety, if possible)
1 cup (2 sticks) unsalted butter, softened
2 tablespoons freshly squeezed lemon juice
½ teaspoon salt
Pinch of white pepper

Put the parsley in the work bowl of a food processor, and mince it fairly fine, using two or three 5-second bursts of power. Combine the parsley with the remaining ingredients, and process the mixture for about 30 seconds, until smooth. Scrape down the work bowl once or twice, and check under the metal blade to make sure the parsley hasn't accumulated under there, then mix once more. Scrape the butter out onto wax paper, and form into two logs. Chill or freeze until firm. Slice off pats of butter as needed.

Mustards

Putting together your own mustard isn't nearly as daunting as it may sound. In fact, it's one of the easier "gourmet" gifts you can whip up. If you don't mention that to people, they will remain forever impressed by your culinary panache. Do take care, however, to find a mustard powder that is agreeable to you—some are quite spicy.

Honey Mustard

A good all-purpose spread, perfect to put into a gift basket of picnic foods.

About ½ cup

½ **cup dry mustard**
2 **tablespoons white wine vinegar**
¼ **cup honey**
2 **tablespoons brown sugar**
½ **teaspoon salt**
⅛ **teaspoon ground cloves**

Combine everything and blend until smooth. Store, covered, in the refrigerator for at least 24 hours before serving.

Miraculous Mustards

While mustard seems like the most natural thing in the world for sandwiches, it's also delicious when used as part of a dip, a dressing, or a marinade. When you give a mustard, encourage your recipient to play around with it, adding it here and there where it seems its flavors could be used. But do include this caution: a little mustard usually goes a long way. Use it sparingly.

Maple-Cinnamon Mustard

A surprising and tasty spiciness sets this special spread apart and makes it a welcome present.

About ⅔ cup

¼ cup cider vinegar
¼ cup firmly packed brown sugar
2 egg yolks (see note)
½ cup dry mustard
¼ cup pure maple syrup
Salt to taste
½ teaspoon ground cinnamon

Mix everything together, and beat until smooth and slightly thickened. Store, tightly covered, in the refrigerator for at least 24 hours before serving.

Note: If you are concerned about the possibility of salmonella bacteria in your eggs, you can set your mind at ease by performing the following pasteurization process: Mix two yolks with 2½ tablespoons of water and 1 teaspoon lemon juice or vinegar in a small custard cup. Cover the cup with plastic wrap and put it in the microwave. Cook on full power until the mixture bubbles, about 45 seconds. Using a clean fork, beat the eggs. Replace the covering, and cook until the mixture bubbles again, about 25 to 30 seconds. Take it out of the microwave, whisk it with another clean fork, and let cool. Use the mixture in place of the 2 egg yolks called for in the recipe.

Cranberry Mustard

It goes without saying that this is the perfect token of appreciation to bring to your Thanksgiving host, whose immediate future likely is chock-full of turkey sandwiches. Do encourage him or her to try it with other meats, though, or as an interesting variant in recipes that call for other mustards.

About ²/₃ cup

1	cup fresh or frozen, thawed cranberries
½	cup dry mustard
¼	cup honey
2	tablespoons cider vinegar
½	teaspoon salt
1	teaspoon grated orange rind

Put the cranberries in a small saucepan with just enough water to cover them. Bring to a boil and let boil until the skins pop, 1 to 2 minutes. Remove from the stove, strain off the liquid, and put the berries through a strainer to remove the skins.

Combine the sieved cranberries with the remaining ingredients and mix until smooth. Cover and store in the refrigerator at least 24 hours before serving.

Stocking the Wild Cranberry

A staple of the Midwest and Northeast, the cranberry is a tangy and versatile bog-grown fruit that is best enjoyed liberally. It's a shame to hoard it for holiday time, as its color and character can be used well throughout the year. Unfortunately, however, the supermarket doesn't share this sentiment, so you must stock up on the friendly berries when they're available. Keeping them couldn't be easier: simply toss the whole bag (if you've bought them in bulk, put them into a plastic bag or other airtight container) into the freezer. When it's time to use the cranberries, just rinse them quickly in cool water and proceed.

Jalapeño Mustard

Not for the faint of heart, this fiery condiment is good to give to those with sturdy palates. It's very tasty with sausages and other meats, but suggest trying it spread on a bagel for a head-clearing taste sensation. And by the way, you needn't tell people how incredibly easy it was to make.

½ cup

 ½ **cup prepared yellow mustard**
 1–3 jalapeños, cored, seeded, and finely chopped

Combine the mustard and peppers; blend well. Store, covered tightly, in the refrigerator.

Italian-Style Mustard

Robust and assertive, this mustard goes well with hearty meats and sausages, though it also is good in sandwiches, dressings, and sauces where its flavorings are compatible. Anyone with a taste for Italian foods will appreciate a jar of this spread.

About ½ cup

½   **cup dry mustard**
4   **teaspoons balsamic vinegar**
2   **teaspoons firmly packed brown sugar**
1   **clove garlic, minced**
2 tablespoons minced fresh basil
4   **teaspoons minced fresh oregano**
Pinch of salt
2   **tablespoons water (or more, to achieve the consistency you like)**

Blend everything together, and stir until smooth. Cover and refrigerate at least 24 hours before serving.

Sweet Treats: Sauces to Satiate

Most of this book is devoted to savory gift-giving ventures, but because humankind does not thrive on mustards and chutneys alone, one must sometimes give thought to the sweet indulgences that end our meals, those forays into richness that trigger the brain's signal to acknowledge satiety. Indeed, numerous dietetic researchers have found evidence that eating something sweet at the end of the meal signals the body that it has had enough. It is to those hard-working nutritional scientists that these two decadent preparations are dedicated.

Peanut Butter–Caramel Dip

Perfect with crisp wedges of apple, this mixture is a good accompaniment to a basket full of freshly picked orchard specimens. It also is delectable with chunks of other fruits speared on toothpicks or morsels of sponge cake. And if you're giving it to a chocolate lover whose sweet tooth knows no bounds, pack it with a couple of bars of high-quality chocolate.

About 1½ cups

¾ **cup smooth peanut butter**
¾ **cup half-and-half**
½ **cup brown sugar**
½ **teaspoon vanilla**

Heat the peanut butter, half-and-half, and brown sugar in a saucepan over medium-high heat until the mixture is bubbly. Let it cook 1 minute at a brisk bubble, stirring it vigorously. Remove the sauce from the heat, and let it cool slightly. Add the vanilla, then beat 1 minute on medium speed of a mixer.

Transfer the dip to a serving container. Let it cool completely, then cover it and chill until ready to use. This dip should be served at room temperature.

Maple Walnut Sauce

It's not exactly a dip or a spread, but this sweet sauce seems to fit in here. A wonderful gift, it can be used to top baked apples, pumpkin pie, rice pudding, bread pudding, or simply as a decadent blanket poured over ice cream.

1 1/2 cups

1¼ cups pure maple syrup
3　tablespoons unsalted butter, cut up, at room temperature
Pinch of salt
¼　cup whipping cream
½　teaspoon vanilla
⅔　cup finely chopped walnuts, toasted lightly

Boil the syrup in a medium, heavy saucepan over medium-high heat until it reaches 240 degrees Fahrenheit on a candy thermometer. Take it off the heat; add the butter, one piece at a time, stirring until the piece melts. Mix in the cream; blend well. Add the vanilla and walnuts. Cool, then place in a covered container and chill. Serve the sauce warm or at room temperature.

THREE ▪ *Dressings and Such*

Salad, that long-neglected pile of greens set off there northwest of the dinner plate, is coming into its own as an exciting, flavorful part of the meal—and almost as often serving as the meal itself. While it's true that part of this may be due to heightened dietary awareness and an increased availability of variety greens, interesting toppings are a big part of the reason as well. You can provide salad dressing that's tastier than anything that's been sitting on the supermarket shelf for a couple of months (or longer), and it will be a much appreciated gift. What's more, you also can put together flavored versions of the most basic of salad dressing components—vinegars and oils—in delicious ways, to enable cooking friends or loved ones to play around with the flavors on their own.

Apple-Mustard Vinaigrette

This hearty variation on basic vinegar and oil can be used with tossed greens or pasta salads. It's particularly nice with meat-enhanced mixtures. And it makes a perfectly respectable marinade. Anything this adaptable makes a great gift.

1³/4 cups

½	cup olive oil
¼	cup cider vinegar
2	tablespoons apple juice or cider
1	tablespoon Dijon mustard
1	large clove garlic, minced
¼	teaspoon fresh thyme

Salt and freshly ground pepper to taste

Whisk all the ingredients together in a bowl, or combine them in a jar, cover it tightly, and shake until the dressing is well blended. Chill.

Lemon-Sesame Vinaigrette

Refreshing and just a touch exotic—good to give to those who like light, delicately flavored foods.

About 1¼ cups

 ¾ cup olive oil
 ¼ cup white wine vinegar
 2 tablespoons freshly squeezed lemon juice
 ½ teaspoon sesame oil
 1 tablespoon toasted sesame seeds
 ½ teaspoon soy sauce, or to taste
 ½ teaspoon grated lemon zest
 1 teaspoon honey
 A few grains cayenne pepper

Mix everything together in a screw-top jar, shaking to blend thoroughly. Keep chilled.

Raspberry-Poppy Seed Vinaigrette

Delicious with poultry or fruit salads, depending on whether you choose chicken stock or apple juice for a base. In the latter case, it's a nice accompaniment for a fruit basket. Keeps about 3 weeks in the refrigerator.

About 1¹/₂ cups

1   cup chicken stock or apple juice
1   teaspoon cornstarch
¼   cup raspberry vinegar (for homemade, see Index for "Basic Flavored Vinegar")
⅓   cup vegetable oil
¼   teaspoon salt
Pinch of white pepper
2   tablespoons poppy seeds

Heat the stock or juice to a boil. Dilute the cornstarch in about 1 tablespoon of cold stock or water and add it to the boiling liquid. Cook, stirring often, until the mixture is thickened slightly. Cool.

Combine the cooled liquid with the vinegar, oil, salt, and pepper in a blender or food processor. Blend on high speed until smooth. Transfer to a covered container, stir in the poppy seeds, and chill until ready to give.

Parmesan Herb Dressing

Tangy and creamy, this mixture is an unusual and refreshing alternative to standard, fattier dressings—a good gift for someone trying to watch fats.

2 cups

½   **medium-sized cucumber**
1   **cup buttermilk**
¼   **cup mayonnaise**
¼   **cup freshly shredded Parmesan cheese**
2   **tablespoons sliced scallions (include some of the green part)**
1   **clove garlic, chopped**
1   **tablespoon Dijon mustard**
1   **tablespoon chopped parsley**
1   **teaspoon lemon juice**
½   **teaspoon dill weed**
Salt and freshly ground pepper to taste

Peel and halve the cucumber lengthwise. Scoop out the seeds, and cut the cucumber into chunks. Put it in a blender or food processor along with the buttermilk, mayonnaise, Parmesan, scallions, garlic, and mustard. Blend or process until smooth. Place it in a container with a cover and stir in the parsley, lemon juice, and dill weed. Taste and adjust seasonings if necessary. Cover tightly and chill.

Golden Blue Cheese Dressing

The boldest of cheeses teams well here with olive oil and plain yogurt for a creamy, substantial topping. Not everyone loves blue cheese, but those who do will savor this dressing.

1³/₄ cups

> ¾ **cup olive oil**
> ⅓ **cup white wine vinegar**
> ⅓ **cup plain yogurt**
> **Salt and freshly ground pepper to taste**
> 1   **cup crumbled blue cheese**

Whisk together the oil, vinegar, yogurt, salt, and pepper until smooth. Stir in the blue cheese. Chill, covered, until ready to use.

Dijon French Dressing

Zesty in character, this dressing is great with tossed greens, but it also serves as a good marinade for either meat or poultry. Its full flavor and elegant name make it a good gift item.

About 2¹/₂ cups

1	cup safflower oil
¾	cup white wine vinegar
¼	cup tomato paste
¼	cup grated onion
1	clove garlic, minced
1	tablespoon Dijon mustard
1	tablespoon horseradish
2	tablespoons honey
1	teaspoon Worcestershire sauce
1	teaspoon salt
½	teaspoon freshly ground pepper

Combine everything in a jar with a screw-on top, seal it up, and shake until well blended. Chill.

Of Vinegars and Oils

Flavored oils and vinegars are perfect for giving to cooks. Their infusions provide a great springboard for the imagination, and they make a handsome gift, with the signature flavor suspended there for all the world to see.

Flavored Oils

Infused oils are a delicious way to add flavor to the things you eat. Almost any herb or spice can be preserved in oil, but it is important to take a few precautions. Most important is to remember that moisture and lack of refrigeration can increase the risk of food poisoning from flavored oils. To limit the amount of water introduced in your oil, avoid overprocessing the additives: don't bruise the garlic, and if you choose to introduce the zip of onions, try using whole small onions rather than larger, chunked-up ones.

And please do be sure to keep the oil well chilled until serving time. Most oils benefit from being brought to room temperature just before use.

Popular uses for flavored oils include brushing on meat before grilling or as ingredients in salad dressings and marinades.

> "For thousands of years the olive tree, its fruit, and its oil have been central to the ritual and the poetic vocabulary, as well as to the eating habits of the Mediterranean region, which is the heart of the civilization of the west. The same oil that is gracing our lettuce salad has been used to bestow irrevocable kingship, to consecrate priests, churches, temples, and holy objects, to light sanctuary lamps, and to signify sacramental grace and strength—even in countries very far away from olive groves and presses. The olive tree is not a spectacular plant, but it is one of the most deeply loved of trees. Contemplating one for the first time, it is not at all obvious why it should have exerted such power over the human imagination."—from *Much Depends on Dinner* by Margaret Visser (Grove Press, 1986).

Basic Flavored Vinegar

There's nothing even a little bit mysterious about those beautiful creations that involve a fresh sprig of herb soaking in vinegar. All it is is a beautiful bottle, a sprig of herbs, and some vinegar. A homemade gift couldn't come easier. But there are a few pointers to keep in mind:

- Use the freshest herbs available. If you haven't an herb garden, find a reliable purveyor of fresh herbs. Place the herb in the bottle, and pour a good white wine vinegar over it, shaking gently to encourage any lingering bubbles to let go. Let the vinegar steep for at least a month before giving it. If you have less time than that, warm the vinegar to just under the boiling point before pouring it over the herb. Take care not to let the vinegar boil, because this will destroy the acetic acid, which is critical for preservation of the herb foliage.

- Cap the bottle securely before setting it in a peaceful spot to steep. Avoid uncoated metal bottle caps, which can react with the vinegar and create an off taste.

- Your featured herb might be more attractive if you replace it with a fresh sprig after the steeping period is up.

- Favorite herbs for preserving in vinegar include basil, tarragon, thyme, dill, rosemary, parsley, and sage—combinations of some of these are particularly nice. Other flavorings you might try: red finger peppers and garlic, threaded on toothpicks or wooden skewers; raspberry, cranberry, or blueberry (use fresh, unblemished berries);

lemon (try floating decoratively sliced rounds in the bottle); fresh currant; or shallot. Or for apple-mint vinegar, try sticking a couple of sprigs of mint into a bottle of cider vinegar.

Basil Oil

Enticingly fragrant, this oil is delicious in dressings or for cooking, but perhaps its virtues are best realized when it's drizzled, slightly warm, over a plate of freshly cooked pasta. It's very very easy to put together, and makes a seemingly extravagant gift.

1 cup

¼ cup coarsely chopped basil
1 cup olive oil

Combine the basil and oil, cover, and refrigerate for at least a week. It can be given with the basil still in it, but I suggest straining it before using. It should be served warm or at room temperature.

Mexican-Style Oil

A robust version of oil, this works well in any Mexican-accented dish. On the gift tag you attach to the bottle, you might suggest brushing it over a burrito and then baking it, to get the feel of a chimichanga, only with less fat and more zip.

2 cups

2	cups olive oil
1	tablespoon chopped cilantro
4	whole garlic cloves, peeled
4	dried red pepper pods

Put the oil and cilantro in a jar. Thread the garlic cloves and pepper pods alternately onto one or two wooden skewers, and place the skewers in the jar with the oil. Cover tightly, and refrigerate for at least a week before using.

FOUR ▪ *Nibblings*

Of course, there's a lot to be said for the ready-to-eat. A gift of food made for munching "as is," be it a finger food or a mixture ready to be spooned from a bowl, is always welcome.Whether your recipient suffers a chronic sweet tooth, is nuts for nuts, or professes a weakness for can't-stop-eating-it foods, there is something delicious you can prepare for a present.

Pesto Pecans

Crisp and habit-forming, these nuts make a gift that is guaranteed to disappear quickly.

4 cups

3   tablespoons butter
½   teaspoon salt
¼   cup Fresh Basil Pesto (see Index)
4   cups pecan halves

Preheat the oven to 325 degrees.

Melt the butter in a large saucepan. Add the salt and pesto; stir until smooth. Take off the heat, mix in the nuts, and toss gently until they are coated.

Spread the nuts in a single layer in a jelly roll pan, scraping any excess pesto goo over them. Bake the nuts for 10 to 12 minutes, stirring two or three times. Cool. Store in an airtight container.

Maple Walnuts

Just a touch of sweetness keeps these nuts in the before-dinner class, though of course they can be nibbled at any time of the day. Flexibility is a trademark of any good gift.

4 cups

¼	cup butter
¼	cup pure maple syrup
2	tablespoons water
1	teaspoon salt
4	cups walnut halves

Preheat the oven to 250 degrees. Line a 10- by 15-inch jelly roll pan with foil.

Combine the butter, syrup, water, and salt in a large saucepan and bring to a boil, stirring constantly. Mix in the nuts; toss gently to coat them.

Spread the nuts in a single layer in the prepared pan. Bake for an hour, stirring every 15 minutes. Spread on wax paper to cool. Break the nuts apart and store in an airtight container.

White Chocolate Trail Mix

A frosty twist on mixed nuts. At Christmastime, it's fun to fold in a few red and green M&M's along with the white chocolate, for a sweet and unusual treat that looks plenty festive when presented in a big glass jar.

10 cups

½ pound white chocolate
2 cups blanched peanuts, roasted and unsalted
1 cup roasted, salted sunflower seeds
2 cups golden raisins
2 cups pretzel sticks, broken up

Break the chocolate into chunks, and set it in a double boiler over simmering water. Melt it slowly, stirring often.

While the chocolate is melting, combine the nuts, raisins, and pretzels in a roaster. Mix well. Pour the melted chocolate over the mixture, and toss until well coated. Spread on wax paper to cool. Break it into pieces, and store in an airtight container.

Maplecorn

The sweet boiled sap of the maple tree does luscious justice to popcorn, making it a treat worthy of giving.

12 cups

3 quarts popped popcorn
½ cup butter
1 cup firmly packed brown sugar
¼ cup pure maple syrup
½ teaspoon salt
¼ teaspoon baking soda
½ teaspoon vanilla
¼ teaspoon maple flavoring

Preheat the oven to 250 degrees. Lightly oil a large roaster or spray it with nonstick cooking spray. Put the popcorn in it and set aside.

In a heavy saucepan, melt the butter over medium-low heat. Stir in the brown sugar, syrup, and salt. Bring to a boil, stirring constantly. Boil without stirring for 5 minutes, moderating the heat just enough to keep the mixture from boiling over. Take off the heat, and stir in the soda and flavorings. Drizzle it over the popcorn; stir with a wooden spoon until evenly coated.

Bake the popcorn for an hour, stirring every 15 minutes. Cool completely, then break into pieces. Store in an airtight container.

Gramma's Herb Toast

My step-grandmother, Frances Chickering, used to make this pleasingly crunchy toast for family gatherings. There never were leftovers.

1   stick butter, softened
Dash of cayenne pepper
½   teaspoon salt
⅓   teaspoon each: paprika, savory, and thyme
1   loaf Pepperidge Farm Veri Thin white bread

Preheat the oven to 225 degrees. Set out two large jelly roll pans.

Cream the butter well, then beat in the seasonings. Spread the mixture very thinly on bread slices. Cut into shapes (triangles, little squares, sticks), and place, in a single layer, on the pans. Bake until dry and crisp, about 1 to 1½ hours. Cool and store in an airtight container.

Pestotoast

A shameless rip-off of Gramma's delicious Herb Toast (the preceding recipe). But I like this variation enough to include it here. And actually, it makes a nice counterpoint to Gramma's preparation, packed up side by side in a nicely decorated basket.

- **1 loaf Pepperidge Farm Veri Thin whole-wheat bread**
- **¼ cup Fresh Basil Pesto (see Index), at room temperature**
- **¼ cup butter, softened**

Preheat the oven to 225 degrees. Set out two large jelly roll pans.

Beat the pesto and butter together until smooth. Spread each slice of bread as thinly as possible with the pesto mixture, then cut the slices into shapes (triangles, little squares, sticks). Place them on the pans in a single layer. Bake until the toast is dry and crisp, about 1 to 1½ hours. Cool and store in an airtight container.

Stovetop Granola

This is the more earthy of the two granolas featured here, the Indian-print-skirted, leather-sandaled yin to the other's Chanel-suited, more continental yang. It's full of fiber and vitamins, and it's a wonderful thing to put in your bowl at breakfast time.

About 5¹/₂ cups, 10 to 12 servings

- ¹/₃ **cup honey**
- ¹/₃ **cup canola oil**
- 4 **cups rolled oats**
- ¹/₂ **cup oat bran**
- ¹/₂ **cup roasted unsalted sunflower meats**
- ¹/₄ **cup sesame seeds**
- 1 **cup raisins or chopped dates**

Heat the honey and oil in a kettle or large saucepan until warm. Stir in the oats, bran, nuts, and sesame seeds; mix well. Cook over medium heat, stirring constantly, until golden, about 15 to 20 minutes. Take off the heat, and cool completely before stirring in the raisins. Store in an airtight container.

Baked Granola

Walnuts and maple syrup are the flavorings used in this lush, easy, and reasonably low-fat mixture. The granola fan on your gift list will love it.

About 6 cups, 12 to 15 servings

4	cups old-fashioned rolled oats
½	cup wheat germ
½	cup unprocessed wheat bran
1	cup (4 ounces) chopped walnuts
1	cup unsweetened flaked coconut
3	tablespoons soy flour (see note)

Pinch of nutmeg

½	cup pure maple syrup
¼	cup vegetable oil
1	teaspoon vanilla

Preheat the oven to 275 degrees.

In a roaster, combine the oats, wheat germ, bran, nuts, coconut, soy flour, and nutmeg. Mix well.

On the stovetop or in the microwave, warm the syrup and oil gently together until they are just tepid. Stir in the vanilla. Drizzle over the oat mixture; toss to coat.

Bake for 30 to 40 minutes, stirring thoroughly every 10 minutes, until golden. Cool, then transfer to an airtight container. Store at room temperature.

Note: Protein-rich soy flour can be found in health food stores.

Sun-Less Dried Tomatoes

Far better than the kind you can buy, home-dried tomatoes make a wonderful gift, particularly if you pair them with some fresh pasta. And your oven works as well as the sun in doing the job of drying them; they retain more of their vibrant scarlet hue, and the flavor is at least as intensely tomato-y. Do keep in mind that if you plan to pack them in oil, they'll need about a month to develop their flavor before they'll be ready to give.

About 3 pints

> 4 pounds fresh, unblemished plum tomatoes
> Salt
> Optional: 12 to 15 medium-sized cloves of garlic, peeled;
>   12 to 15 fresh basil leaves; 2 cups olive oil

Preheat the oven to 140 degrees. Put a large piece of aluminum foil on the lower rack of your oven.

Slice the tomatoes in half lengthwise and scoop out their seeds. Salt the cut surfaces lightly and place the tomatoes, cut side up, on a rack placed just above the one with the foil on it. Leave them in the oven until they are dried out and leathery, but not yet crisp. This will take anywhere from 12 to 18 hours, depending on the peculiarities of your oven. Check them often.

Once cooled, the tomatoes can be put into a little bag and given as they are, or they can be packed into jars this way: Put a layer of tomatoes on the bottom, then drop in a garlic clove and a basil leaf. Put in another layer of tomatoes and continue this way until they are all used up. Pour olive oil carefully over the top layer until the mixture is completely covered. Jiggle the jar(s) gently to jostle out any air pockets. Seal the jar(s) tightly and store in the refrigerator for about 4 weeks before giving them.

Bell Pepper Sludge

Perfect to make and give away when the harvest brings a rainbow of peppers to the local market, this colorful mixture can be made part of an antipasto platter, served up with slices of mozzarella cheese and olives and perhaps a sausage or two.

1 quart

6   **large bell peppers (use at least three colors: red, green, yellow, orange, purple, and/or black)**
6   **large cloves garlic, cut into slivers**
Salt and freshly ground pepper
1   **lemon, cut in half**
1   **cup olive oil**

Preheat the broiler. Cut the peppers in half and remove the cores, veins, and seeds. Place them, cut surfaces down, on a large baking sheet, and place under the broiler until the skin is charred all over, about 5 to 7 minutes, but watch them carefully. When they are blackened, pop them into a brown paper bag, crimp its top and let them sit in there for 10 minutes or so, to steam the skins loose. Then pull off the skins with the help of a paring knife. Be sure to remove all specks of charred skin.

Cut the peppers lengthwise into ½-inch strips. Place a layer of peppers, using equal amounts of each color, in the bottom of one quart-size or two pint-size jars. Sprinkle on a few slivers of garlic, a little salt, a grinding of pepper, and a squeeze (a few drops) of lemon juice. Repeat the layers until everything is used up, then pour olive oil over the whole creation. Shake the jar(s) gently to coax out any air bubbles trapped among the peppers. Seal the jar(s) securely, and store in the refrigerator until it's time to give the peppers away.

For Love of Peppers

The late Laurie Colwin, novelist and food philosopher, and her love of red bell peppers were the inspiration for Bell Pepper Sludge. Her book, *Home Cooking* (Knopf, 1988), is wonderful inspiration for any cook, especially the sort who loves to cook for others.

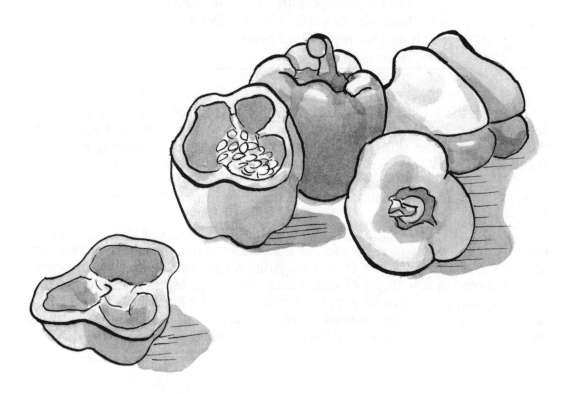

FIVE · *Lotsa Pasta*

A delicious and always welcome gift, pasta is surprisingly easy to make, and it lends itself well to a wide variety of variations. It's also wonderful to give in combination with toppings and flavored oils and vinegars.

While the mixtures and doughs are user-friendly, a few basic pointers are called for before you begin. So here begins Pasta 101: Introduction to the Noodle. It applies generally to manual pasta makers and should be helpful to those whose machines did not come with comprehensive how-tos.

In these recipes, semolina flour is used, sometimes along with regular unbleached white flour. The semolina gives your pasta protein and a good firm texture, and the inclusion of regular flour makes some doughs a bit easier to handle. If you have trouble finding semolina flour in the supermarket, try a health food store or a bulk foods store.

Generally, pasta making involves the dry mixture and the wet. The flour and any additional dry flavorings that are to be included in the pasta are mixed together, either directly on the working surface—ideally a big wooden pastry board—or in a large bowl. Make a well in the center of the dry mixture and set it aside.

You can mix the wet ingredients together in a bowl or directly in the well in the dry ingredients, depending on how dexterous you're feeling. If there are several wet components to be combined, it's probably better to do the beating within the more forgiving confines of a mixing bowl. Pour the wet mixture into the well, and mix in the dry ingredients, bit by bit, with a fork. When a dough begins to form, let your hands jump in and take over. Knead the dough a few times, working on a lightly floured surface, then gather up any stray bits of half-mixed ingredients (a pastry scraper is handy here) and discard them. Continue kneading the dough until it is firm, uniformly combined, and most of the stickiness is gone. Poke a finger into the middle of the mass to check the sticky factor.

Once the dough is well mixed, cover it with a damp kitchen towel so it won't dry out as you work with it one piece at a time. Cut off a lump of dough about the size of an egg, using your pastry scraper or a dull knife. Run it through the rollers on the pasta machine, set on the widest-open setting. If it retains any sticky feel at all, fold the dough in half and run it through once or twice more. Then move the rollers one setting closer together and run the dough through (don't fold it anymore). Continue rolling it through, moving the rollers one notch closer together each time, until you reach the desired thinness. The setting just before the thinnest one usually suffices, though sometimes you might want the pasta particularly thin and delicate.

As you finish rolling out the sheets, set them aside on a drying rack or wooden board to dry a bit. But keep moving—the dough won't cut well if it's allowed to dry out too much. Once all the dough is rolled out, cut it into the widths you want, either by using the cutters that accompany the machine or by rolling up the sheets and cutting them into strips with a knife. If the pasta is going to be given and eaten soon, pack it loosely into a plastic bag and refrigerate it. Otherwise, separate the strands as best you can and let them hang to dry. Or, for more convenient gift giving, divide them into small handfuls and coil them loosely. Be sure to allow plenty of time for the noodles to dry completely before packing them airtight in plastic bags or wide-mouth jars. Dried pasta should be stored at room temperature.

Homemade pasta usually cooks up faster than the dry boxed stuff from the store. If it's very fresh—still moist or just barely dried—it might take as little as a minute or two in a kettle of briskly boiling water. Longer-dried noodles can cook in 5 minutes or so. Check early and often as it cooks to avoid the dismal prospect of overcooked pasta. You might make a note of these cooking guidelines on a pretty tag tied to your homemade gift noodles.

Tomato Pesto Pasta

Perfect pasta partners unite as flavorings for the very noodles themselves. This highly presentable pasta is delicious all alone, or maybe tossed with some olive oil and freshly shredded Parmesan, but it also makes great lasagna.

1 pound

2	cups semolina flour
½	teaspoon salt
2	eggs
2	tablespoons tomato paste
¼	cup Fresh Basil Pesto (see Index)
1	tablespoon water

Please read the basic pasta instructions in the introduction to this chapter. Combine the semolina flour and salt, and make a well in the mixture.

In a small bowl, beat the eggs, tomato paste, pesto, and water together with a fork, mixing thoroughly. Add to the well in the dry mixture, and knead, roll, cut, dry, and store as directed.

Lemon-Pepper Pasta

This refreshing flavor complements grilled fish well, particularly when served with a sauce well suited to both foods. Adaptable enough to be part of many different gift assortments, it's also good tossed with a combination of chopped broccoli, red bell pepper, garlic, and cheese.

1 pound

1¼ cups semolina flour
¾ cup unbleached all-purpose flour
2 teaspoons freshly ground black pepper (finely ground; sieve if necessary)
1 teaspoon salt
3 eggs
1 tablespoon freshly squeezed lemon juice
½ teaspoon lemon extract

Please read the basic pasta instructions in the introduction to this chapter. Combine the flours, pepper, and salt, and make a well.

Beat the eggs, lemon juice, and lemon extract together, mixing well. Add to the well in the dry mixture and knead, roll, cut, dry, and store the pasta as directed.

Mushroom-Garlic-Rosemary Pasta

Richly brown in hue and unusual in flavor, this robust noodle stands up well to a no-nonsense sauce—Alfredo is good—and a sturdy wine. Both of those items go nicely with this pasta in a gift collection.

1 pound

2	cups semolina flour
2	tablespoons mushroom powder (see note)
2	teaspoons granulated garlic
2	teaspoons ground rosemary
½	teaspoon salt
3	eggs
1	tablespoon olive oil

Please read the basic pasta instructions in the introduction to this chapter. Combine the semolina flour, mushroom powder, garlic, rosemary, and salt, and make a well in the middle of the mixture.

Beat the eggs and olive oil together, and add to the dry mixture. Knead, roll, cut, dry, and store as directed.

Note: Mushroom powder, made from ground dried mushrooms, can be found in some herb shops and bulk grocery stores, or check "Sources" (Part V).

Spinach-Nutmeg Pasta

The subtle company of nutmeg works nicely with spinach in this all-purpose pasta.

1 pound

2	cups semolina flour
2	tablespoons spinach powder (see note)
½	teaspoon nutmeg (preferably freshly grated)
½	teaspoon salt
3	eggs

Please read the basic pasta instructions in the introduction to this chapter. Combine the semolina flour, spinach powder, nutmeg, and salt, and make a well in the mixture.

Break the eggs into the well, and mix them in, then knead, roll, cut, dry, and store the pasta as directed.

Note: Spinach powder, made from pulverized dried spinach, is sold in some herb shops and bulk grocery stores, or check "Sources" (Part V).

Dijon-Herb Pasta

Good tossed with freshly steamed vegetables, maybe a touch of pesto, some olive oil, and freshly shredded Parmesan or Romano cheese. This is a distinctively flavored pasta, well suited to giving.

1 pound

1   cup unbleached white flour
1   cup semolina flour
½   teaspoon salt
1   teaspoon dried basil or oregano
½   teaspoon dried thyme
¼   teaspoon dried marjoram
2   eggs
1½ tablespoons Dijon mustard

Please read the basic pasta instructions in the introduction to this chapter. Combine the flours, salt, and herbs. Make a well in the center of the mixture.

Mix the eggs and mustard together in a small bowl, and combine with the dry ingredients, then knead, roll, cut, dry, and store the pasta as directed.

SIX ▪ *Libations*

Time tested and nearly always accepted gratefully, special libations make good gifts, particularly when you've made them yourself. They bring extra cause for celebration.

With many of us cutting back on alcohol consumption these days, the concept of the beverage has taken on new possibilities. Juices have nearly limitless potential for tasty combinations, and tea also makes an ideal springboard for your libation imagination.

Of course, lots of folks still consider a spirited beverage to be a good gift. For these people consider something rich and traditional or a mixture just a touch out of the ordinary. And then raise your glass and think of a good toast (or write one on the gift tag). Cheers!

Irish Cream

Lush and satisfying, this easy mixture is the perfect host/hostess gift to bring to help finish off a special meal. I think it tastes better than the brand-name stuff, and it has less than half the fat.

4 cups

1⅓ cups Scotch
1   cup milk
1   14-ounce can sweetened condensed milk
2   tablespoons chocolate syrup
2   teaspoons instant coffee powder
1   teaspoon vanilla
½   teaspoon almond extract

Combine everything in a blender or mixing bowl, and blend until thoroughly combined. Transfer to one or more tightly covered containers, and chill several hours at least. Shake well before serving.

Coffee Liqueur

A little bit of advance planning is needed for this richly flavored mixture, because it needs to sit for 2 weeks before it can be given away. It's good all alone, over ice, with milk or cream, or poured over ice cream.

About ¹/₂ gallon

4   cups water
2   cups sugar
1   cup instant coffee powder
1   750-ml. bottle 100-proof vodka
Vanilla beans

Boil the water, then add the sugar and coffee, stir well, and boil again. Cool the liquid, then put it into a larger container if necessary, and stir in the vodka. Put a vanilla bean in the bottom of each bottle (if there are several, use half a vanilla bean in each one), then add the liqueur, seal the bottles securely, and let them sit for 2 weeks, stirring or gently shaking them occasionally.

Mint Liqueur

Refreshing and different, this is a gracious gift for those who like to savor life's delicate flavors. Like the Coffee Liqueur, it needs some lead time before it's ready to give.

2¹/₂ cups

> 3   tablespoons coarsely chopped fresh peppermint leaves
> 3   or 4 pieces of orange rind, about ½ inch by 3 inches
>   (orange part only)
> 1   pint brandy
> ¼   cup water
> ¼   cup honey

Combine the mint leaves, rind, and brandy in a bottle with a cork. Let steep 2 to 3 weeks, then strain the liquid.

Bring the water to a boil in a small saucepan. Take it off the heat, stir in the honey, and mix the syrup well. Let it cool slightly, then stir it into the liqueur. Let the liqueur sit another 2 weeks or longer before presenting it.

Plum Brandy

When the local plum crop is sweet and ripe, this is a great way to preserve its essence to share on another day. It will take about 6 weeks to complete the distilling process, so plan ahead.

About 6 cups

1	pound ripe red or purple plums
2	cups sugar
4	cups vodka

Pierce each plum in several places with a sharp-tined fork. Put them into a large glass jar with a snug lid.

Stir the sugar and vodka together and pour the mixture over the plums. Cover.

Leave the container in a cool place out of direct sunlight. Shake the jar gently every 2 to 3 days for 6 weeks. When the 6 weeks have passed, take out the plums, strain the liqueur into one or more decorative bottles, adorn with trimmings, and give.

Sangría

If you're invited to someone's house for tapas—those little portions of savory Spanish delights—bring along a bottle of this congenial beverage. Meant for serving in tall glasses over ice, it hails from the home turf of King Ferdinand and Queen Isabella. All those explorers, and now this! Thanks, your majesties.

About 7 cups

1	1.5-liter bottle dry red wine (a Spanish variety, if possible)
4	teaspoons sugar
½	cup Cointreau
½	cup brandy (a Spanish variety, if possible)
1	lemon, thinly sliced, seeds removed
2	oranges, thinly sliced, seeds removed

Mix the wine and sugar together in a large bowl, and stir until the sugar dissolves. Add the Cointreau, brandy, and fruit. Transfer to one or more tightly lidded bottles or jars, and chill until ready to give.

Hot Spiced Wine

Ready to heat and enjoy, this tasty mixture is a good wintertime gift.

About 8 servings

1	long stick cinnamon, broken into 1-inch pieces
¼	teaspoon ground cloves
¼	teaspoon freshly grated nutmeg
¼	cup freshly squeezed lemon juice
½	cup honey
1	750-ml. bottle dry red wine
1	cup port wine

Combine everything and place the mixture in one or more decorative bottles. Cork securely.

To serve, simply warm over moderate heat. Strain into mugs and serve hot, garnished with thin slices of lemon studded with whole cloves, if desired.

Wassail

The quintessential yuletide libation, this sweet mixture is designed for sharing. Just one taste and you'll understand what inspired the lyrics "Love and joy come to you, and to you good wassail, too."

Almost a gallon

1	quart cranberry juice
5	cups orange juice
2	tablespoons sugar
½	teaspoon allspice
¼	teaspoon ground cloves
1	1.5-liter bottle Sauternes

Mix the cranberry juice, orange juice, sugar, allspice, and cloves in a large kettle or Dutch oven. Heat almost to a simmer, then remove from the heat, cool slightly, and stir in the Sauternes. Cool and chill.

To serve, heat the mixture very gently—do not let it boil. Ladle into cups, garnished with a slice of orange studded with whole cloves, if desired.

Mulled Berry Cider

For those who live in wintry climes, this sweet and spicy mixture is nice to present in a bottle with a big, perfect apple tethered colorfully to its neck. The apple is to be cut into slices for floating atop each steamy mug of cider.

About 10 cups

2 quarts (64 ounces) apple cider
1 pint fresh strawberries, washed, hulled, and sliced, or raspberries (10 ounces frozen unsweetened berries may be substituted)
1 4-inch cinnamon stick
25 whole cloves
¼ teaspoon nutmeg

Combine the cider, berries, and spices in a large saucepan. Heat to a boil; reduce the heat, cover, and simmer for about 10 minutes. Strain the mixture and cool. Transfer to an airtight container and chill until ready to give.

To serve, heat gently and ladle into mugs. Float an apple slice atop each serving.

Spiced Fruit Tea

A refreshing twist on tea, this warm beverage can help chase away the late-winter blues. That's a nice gift to give.

1 gallon

1   cup sugar
20 whole cloves
Water
6   tea bags (standard black tea)
6   cups boiling water
6   cups cold water
3   cups orange juice
2   cups pineapple juice
½   cup fresh lemon juice

In a small saucepan, combine the sugar and cloves. Add enough water to cover and heat gently until the sugar has melted.

In a kettle or Dutch oven, mix the tea bags with 6 cups boiling water, and let steep for 3 hours. Pour in 6 cups cold water, and take out the tea bags. Add the sugar/clove mixture to the kettle and bring to a boil. Take off the heat; stir in the orange, pineapple, and lemon juices. Strain the mixture into one or more large glass jars or bottles, and chill until ready to give.

To serve, heat the tea very gently—do not let it boil. Ladle into mugs and serve, garnished with a slice of lemon, orange, or pineapple, if desired.

Cranberry-Orange Twist

A refreshing combination, good for giving at holiday time or whenever you're looking for something a little unusual.

About 3 cups

1	cup cranberries
¼	cup water
2	cups orange juice (with pulp)
2	tablespoons honey

Combine the cranberries and water in a small saucepan and cook over medium heat until the berries' skins pop and their pulp is quite soft, about 4 to 6 minutes. Stir often. Take off the heat, cool slightly, and then push through a strainer into a blender. Add the orange juice and honey, and whirl the mixture until smooth. Transfer to a jar or bottle, and chill until ready to give.

Apple-Strawberry Juice

This is a good gift for families with little kids, but remember that berry allergies are common—when in doubt, ask. If you live in an area where strawberries are grown, try making this when the picking season is at a peak—the fruit is unbelievably sweet and flavorful, and you can feel free to use extra-ripe or otherwise less-than-perfect berries in this juice.

About 1 quart

> 2 **cups fresh strawberries, washed and hulled**
> 2 **cups apple juice (preferably unfiltered)**
> ¼ **teaspoon nutmeg**

Combine the berries, juice, and nutmeg in a blender and whirl together until smooth. Strain into one or more jars or bottles with tight lids. Chill thoroughly before giving.

Bloody Mary Mixer

There's something artful about a perfect Bloody Mary: a delicate balance of tartness and spice. Whether you choose to add vodka or not, this preparation makes the classic brunch-time cocktail easily accessible.

About 2 quarts

4	cups tomato juice
3	cups V-8 Juice
⅓	cup freshly squeezed lemon juice
¼	cup Worcestershire sauce
1	to 2 teaspoons Tabasco sauce
1	teaspoon celery salt
1	teaspoon freshly ground pepper

   Mix everything together. Transfer the mixture to bottles or jars with tight covers. Chill thoroughly before using.

Bloody Good Cocktail

The route to the perfect Bloody Mary certainly has been the topic of more than one heated debate, and perhaps a war or two. In fact, there are many ways to make a pleasing tomato juice–based cocktail; this is just one. As to garnishing the mixture, it might do to suggest to your recipient some embellishments, maybe even including them with the mix and a bottle of spirits, if appropriate. Some folks, in lieu of the standard slice of lime and/or celery rib, opt for a dill pickle spear to function as their swizzle stick. At The Corral, a great bar and restaurant in Montana's Gallatin Canyon, they garnish their legendary bloodies with an assemblage of pickled asparagus, a spiced green bean, a dill pickle, and a pepperoncini, all speared together. Similarly, what you add to the mix is a matter of preference. Vodka is the traditional liquor, but some people like gin or tequila better. For a surprisingly tasty combination, you might suggest adding a few drops of brandy and tequila along with the vodka. And of course, there's nothing wrong with encouraging people to enjoy the mix all alone, for a wholesome, tasty, and liquor-free refreshment. You might even write and construct a pretty recipe booklet listing these variations and tie it to the mix.

Lemonade

Nothing seems more appropriate for toasting the lazy days of summer than home-made lemonade. So it follows that it's also a great gift to bestow in the midst of dog days.

1 quart

¼ cup pure maple syrup
Zest of 1 lemon, removed with a paring knife
    (yellow part only)
1 cup hot tap water
½ cup freshly squeezed lemon juice (2 or 3 lemons' worth)
3 cups cold water

Combine the syrup, lemon zest, and 1 cup hot tap water. Stir well. Let the mixture sit for a few minutes while you squeeze the lemons.

Strain the syrup mixture into a quart-size jar or a pitcher, then stir in 3 cups of cold water and the lemon juice. Chill before serving.

SEVEN ▪ *Mixing It Up: For the Cook Who Has Everything*

Not so long ago, the idea of giving someone a dry mix for a present would not have struck a gracious chord. Think of gift giving, and chances are Duncan Hines and Betty Crocker aren't the first names that come to mind. But as most of us know, times are changing.

Offering a gift of a mix is more than simply presenting some food that still needs work. What you're really doing when you give your friends delicious food that's partially made is enabling them to enjoy that food perfectly fresh and homemade whenever they're ready to do so, without having to put out all the time and effort required of cooking from scratch. You're giving them the best gift of all: more time to spend with people they like, enjoying the things they really like to do. These days there aren't many of us who have too much of that on our hands.

These recipes all are printed with the directions needed to make the mix. Instructions for preparing the finished products, which you'll need to include with each mix, are marked with and appear after each mix recipe. Given together in a little hand-lettered cookbooklet along with the mix or on pretty index cards, these recipes make nice corollary gifts. Remember to include the recipe yields.

Buttermilk Baking Mix

The basic, 1,001-dishes-in-a-box baking mix still provides cooks with the greatest number of options. It's likely that most cooks you know already have a few recipes in their files in which this wholesome and all-purpose mix can be used. We go through a lot of this at our house, from quick breakfast muffins to dinner pies to tiny cheese biscuits mixed up and baked in my daughter's E-Z Bake Oven. It makes good camping provisions, because a little mix and water (three parts mix to one part water) is all it takes to whip up fresh biscuits. The seven recipes that follow this one, from Charlie P's Pancakes through the recipe for Apple Granola Muffins, all use the Buttermilk Baking Mix and can accompany the mix as part of your gift. Each of them has a next to the recipe title to indicate the recipe itself makes a great gift!

- 4 **cups unbleached all-purpose flour**
- ½ **cup wheat germ**
- ½ **cup unprocessed wheat bran or oat bran**
- ½ **cup dry buttermilk**
- 2 **tablespoons baking powder**
- 1 **tablespoon baking soda**
- 1 **teaspoon salt**
- ¼ **cup vegetable shortening**

Combine the flour, wheat germ, bran, buttermilk powder, baking powder, baking soda, and salt in the work bowl of a food processor. Mix until well blended. Distribute the shortening over the surface of the dry mixture in blobs. Mix it in, scraping the bowl once or twice to make sure it's blended.

Transfer the mix to a storage container with a tight-fitting lid, and keep in the refrigerator or freezer until needed.

✑ Charlie P.'s Pancakes

Using the Buttermilk Baking Mix, my brother-in-law Charlie Petoskey does up a wicked batch of cholesterol-lowering pancakes.

4 to 6 servings

2	cups Buttermilk Baking Mix
3	egg whites
1½	cups skim milk
½	cup oat bran
1	ripe banana

Mix everything in a blender, after layering the ingredients alternately to prevent the blender blades from mucking up too much, until the batter is smooth.

Cook the pancakes on a lightly oiled griddle until they are golden on both sides. Serve with warm maple syrup.

❧ Cheesy Chicken Pot Pie

Here's another recipe to accompany your packages of Buttermilk Baking Mix. Simultaneously rich and wholesome, this vegetable-packed pie offers up the best that "comfort foods" have to give. Don't be deterred by the long list of ingredients; this isn't a difficult dish to put together.

6 to 8 servings

5   tablespoons butter
½   cup chopped onion
¼   cup finely chopped celery
¼   cup shredded carrot
¼   cup flour
1¼ cups milk, divided
¾   cup chicken stock (preferably homemade)
2   tablespoons chopped parsley
¾   teaspoon chopped fresh thyme, or ¼ teaspoon dried
Salt and freshly ground pepper to taste
3   ounces cream cheese or Neufchâtel cheese, cut into pieces
¼   cup freshly grated Parmesan cheese
1½ cups chopped broccoli
3   cups diced, cooked chicken
1   cup Buttermilk Baking Mix
1   cup shredded Cheddar cheese
1 egg, lightly beaten
1   tablespoon vegetable oil
¼   cup sliced almonds

Preheat the oven to 375 degrees. Lightly butter a 2-quart baking dish.

Melt the butter in a medium saucepan; sauté the onion, celery, and carrot over medium heat until softened. Stir in the flour and cook, stirring, for a minute or two, until the flour starts to turn golden. Add ¾ cup of the milk, the stock, parsley, thyme, salt, and pepper; cook, stirring constantly, until the liquid is thickened. Reduce the heat to low and stir in the cream cheese and Parmesan; stir until they melt. Mix in the broccoli and chicken. Pour the mixture into the prepared baking dish.

Combine the baking mix and Cheddar in a mixing bowl. Beat the egg, oil, and the remaining ½ cup of milk together and add to the dry mixture. Beat with a fork for about 30 seconds, until a soft dough is formed. Spread the dough over the vegetable mixture in the dish. Sprinkle the top with sliced almonds.

Bake the pie for 20 to 25 minutes, until the top is golden and the filling is bubbly.

🕱 Caramel-Pecan Streusel Ring

A good, sticky coffee cake that uses the Buttermilk Baking Mix.

4 to 6 servings

> 5 tablespoons butter or margarine, divided
> ¼ cup firmly packed brown sugar
> ¼ cup chopped pecans
> 2 tablespoons light corn syrup
> 2 cups Buttermilk Baking Mix
> ½ cup milk
> 1 egg
> Streusel (recipe follows)

Preheat the oven to 400 degrees. Butter a 6-cup ring mold.

In a little saucepan or microwave-safe bowl, mix 2 tablespoons of the butter with the brown sugar, pecans, and corn syrup. Heat on the stovetop or in the microwave until bubbly, stirring once or twice. Pour it into the prepared pan, spreading the mixture evenly.

Mix the baking mix with the milk and egg; beat briskly with a fork for about 30 seconds to form a soft dough. Spoon the dough in blobs evenly around the ring.

Melt the remaining 3 tablespoons of butter and drizzle it over the dough. Sprinkle on the streusel.

Bake the coffee cake for 12 to 15 minutes, until a wooden toothpick inserted near the center comes out clean. Immediately invert the cake onto a warm serving platter. Serve warm.

Streusel:

Mix ¼ cup chopped pecans, 2 tablespoons sugar, and ½ teaspoon cinnamon in a small bowl.

~ Parmesan Herb Biscuits

Your appreciative family and friends will use your Buttermilk Baking Mix often to make these savory, easy-to-make biscuits. They are best with fresh herbs, but you can use dried oregano and thyme if necessary.

12 to 16 biscuits

2¼ cups Buttermilk Baking Mix
⅓ cup freshly grated Parmesan cheese
2 medium-sized scallions, minced
2 teaspoons minced fresh oregano, or ½ teaspoon dried
1 teaspoon minced fresh thyme leaves, or ¼ teaspoon dried
1 tablespoon minced fresh parsley
⅔ cup milk

Preheat the oven to 450 degrees.

Combine the mix, cheese, scallions, and herbs in a medium mixing bowl. Stir in the milk and stir briskly, for about 30 seconds, to form a soft dough. Turn the dough out onto a board that is generously dusted with baking mix; knead 10 times. Pat the dough out to an even ½-inch thickness; cut with a floured cutter. Place the rounds on an ungreased baking sheet and bake for 8 to 10 minutes, until golden. Serve warm.

Pumpkin-Oat Bran Muffins

A tasty and nutritious breakfast treat.

12 muffins

1¾ cups Buttermilk Baking Mix
¾ cup oat bran
¾ cup firmly packed brown sugar
2 teaspoons cinnamon
⅓ cup vegetable oil
1 cup pumpkin puree (homemade or canned)
3 eggs
½ cup raisins (optional)

Preheat the oven to 400 degrees. Lightly oil 12 muffin tins, or line them with cupcake papers.

Combine the mix, oat bran, sugar, and cinnamon in a mixing bowl, blending with fingertips to mix thoroughly. Beat the oil, pumpkin, and eggs together, and add to the dry mixture; blend well. Stir in the raisins.

Fill the prepared muffin tins three-quarters of the way up with batter. Bake for 15 to 18 minutes.

Note: For a variation, try substituting applesauce or an apple-fruit sauce for the pumpkin. Reduce the sugar to ½ cup.

# Raisin Bran Muffins

Breakfast cereal doesn't necessarily have to be eaten out of a bowl.

8 muffins

1½ cups raisin bran cereal
¾   cup milk
1   cup Buttermilk Baking Mix
⅓   cup sugar
2   tablespoons melted butter
1   egg
½   teaspoon cinnamon
Cinnamon sugar (optional)

Preheat the oven to 400 degrees. Line 8 muffin tins with cupcake papers.

Pour the milk over the cereal in a large bowl. Let the mixture sit for 3 to 5 minutes. Add the remaining ingredients except the cinnamon sugar, and beat well. Spoon the batter into the prepared tins. Sprinkle the tops with cinnamon sugar, if desired. Bake the muffins for 20 to 25 minutes, until golden. Serve warm.

Apple-Granola Muffins

Another of the cereal-gone-muffin genre.

8 muffins

2	egg whites
1	cup Buttermilk Baking Mix
½	cup milk
1	small apple, peeled, cored, and chopped (about ½ cup)
1	tablespoon vegetable oil
1	teaspoon cinnamon
⅓	cup granola
3	tablespoons sugar

Preheat the oven to 400 degrees. Lightly oil 8 muffin tins or line them with cupcake papers.

Beat the egg whites lightly; mix in the remaining ingredients. Fill the prepared muffin tins about two-thirds of the way up. Bake for 15 to 17 minutes.

Whole-Grain Pancake Mix

More specialized than the buttermilk mix above, this hearty blend makes pancake breakfasts an easy thing to achieve—and thus a great gift to give.

About 6 cups, enough for 50 to 60 pancakes

2⅔ cups whole-wheat flour
1⅓ cups unbleached all-purpose flour
1   cup oat flour (see note)
½   cup wheat germ
3   tablespoons sugar
1   cup powdered buttermilk (see note)
4   teaspoons baking powder
2   teaspoons baking soda
1   teaspoon salt

Combine all the ingredients well, and store in an airtight container in the refrigerator or freezer.

Note: If you can't find oat flour at the store, try making your own by pulverizing uncooked rolled oats in a food processor. Also, you may omit the buttermilk powder, but be sure to adjust the pancake directions to include 1 cup of plain yogurt in place of the water, plus milk as needed to thin the batter to the desired consistency.

For 12 to 15 pancakes, combine 1½ cups mix with 1 cup water, 1 egg, 1 tablespoon vegetable oil, and ¼ teaspoon vanilla. Mix well and cook on a lightly greased griddle over medium heat until golden brown.

Ginger Muffin Mix

A refreshing spiciness distinguishes these golden muffins, whipped up easily when you've prepared this mix for a gift.

12 muffins

2	cups unbleached all-purpose flour
1	tablespoon baking powder
½	teaspoon baking soda
½	teaspoon salt
¼	cup nonfat dry milk
¼	cup sugar
1½	teaspoons ground ginger
1	teaspoon cinnamon
¼	teaspoon ground nutmeg
¼	teaspoon ground cloves
2	tablespoons vegetable oil

Mix the flour, baking powder, baking soda, salt, dry milk, sugar, and spices in a food processor or mixer. Dribble in the oil and mix well. Store in a cool, dry place. If it's not to be used soon, it can be stored in the refrigerator.

To make a dozen muffins, preheat the oven to 400 degrees. Lightly oil 12 muffin tins, or line them with cupcake papers.

Combine the mix with ¾ cup milk and 1 egg. Beat swiftly with a wooden spoon for 30 seconds. Spoon the batter into the prepared pan, filling each tin about two-thirds of the way up. Bake for 15 minutes or until golden brown.

Hawaiian Muffin Mix

This unusual mix makes a batch of 12 refreshing little cakes that can be used to transport a dreary February afternoon to a place where palm trees sway in the breeze and the sun always shines. Nice gift.

12 muffins

2   **cups cake flour**
2   **tablespoons sugar**
1   **teaspoon baking powder**
½   **teaspoon baking soda**
½   **teaspoon salt**
½   **cup chopped sweetened dried pineapple**
⅓   **cup unsweetened coconut**

Sift the flour, sugar, baking powder, baking soda, and salt together. Stir in the pineapple and coconut. Store at room temperature in an airtight container.

To make a dozen muffins, first preheat the oven to 400 degrees. Beat ¾ cup buttermilk with 3 tablespoons melted, slightly cooled butter, 1 beaten egg, and 2 tablespoons of dark rum. Stir the liquid into the mix, stirring only until the dry parts are moistened. Spoon into lightly buttered or paper-lined muffin tins, filling each one about two-thirds full. Bake for 20 to 25 minutes, until the muffins are lightly golden brown.

Applesauce-Oatmeal Muffin Mix

Here's a wholesome, homemade spin-off of those boxed mixes that comes with a little jar of secret goo to add to the batter. If you give it as a gift, it's especially nice to include some Basic Applesauce (see Index).

24 muffins

2	cups rolled oats
1½	cups unbleached all-purpose flour
1½	cups whole-wheat flour
2	teaspoons baking soda
2	teaspoons baking powder
1	teaspoon salt
2	teaspoons ground cinnamon
1	teaspoon ground cloves
1	cup raisins
2	cups applesauce (preferably homemade and unsweetened, see Index for "Basic Applesauce")

Combine the oats, flours, baking soda, baking powder, salt, and spices. Stir in the raisins. Transfer to an airtight container and store at room temperature. Package the applesauce separately, and present the pair with the following recipe:

☞ To make a dozen muffins, first preheat the oven to 375 degrees. Lightly oil 12 muffins tins or line them with cupcake papers.

In a large bowl, beat 1 cup of the applesauce with ½ cup firmly packed dark brown sugar, 2 eggs, and ½ cup vegetable oil. Measure out half of the mix and add it to the applesauce mixture, stirring just until everything is combined.

Spoon the batter into the prepared tins, and bake for 20 to 25 minutes, until a wooden toothpick inserted in the center of one of the muffins comes out clean. Cool on a rack.

Pecan Muffin Mix

Not too sweet, these muffins go as well with supper as they do with brunch.

12 muffins

1	cup chopped pecans
1	cup unbleached all-purpose flour
¾	cup whole-wheat flour
2	teaspoons baking powder
¼	teaspoon baking soda
½	teaspoon salt

Put the pecans in a small, dry skillet over medium-high heat. Toast, stirring constantly, until the nuts are lightly golden brown and fragrant. Take from the heat, and spread on a small piece of paper towel to cool.

Stir the flours, baking powder, baking soda, and salt together with a fork. Mix in the cooled pecans. Transfer to an airtight container and store at room temperature.

To make a dozen muffins, first preheat the oven to 400 degrees. Lightly oil 12 muffin tins, or line them with cupcake papers.

In a medium bowl, lightly beat 1 large egg. Stir in ⅓ cup honey, ½ cup milk, and ¼ cup vegetable oil. Blend in the dry mix, stirring just until the dry ingredients are moistened.

Spoon the batter into the prepared tins, filling each about two-thirds of the way up. Bake for 18 to 20 minutes.

Scone Mix

Utterly civilized, the versatile scone has come to feel at home on breakfast tables and tea carts alike. It's nice to be able to make them quickly and easily, which is possible with this mix on hand.

8 cups, enough for 32 scones

8	cups unbleached all-purpose flour
2	tablespoons baking powder
1	tablespoon baking soda
6	tablespoons sugar
½	teaspoon salt

Combine everything and mix well. Store in an airtight container.

 To make 16 scones, first preheat the oven to 375 degrees. Butter two baking sheets.

Shake the mix to recombine it. Put 4 cups into a mixing bowl.

Beat 1 egg, 1 cup buttermilk, and ½ cup melted butter together. Work into the dry mixture with a fork, then blend lightly with your hands to make a dough. Without handling the dough too much, pat it out ½-inch thick on a floured board. Cut into 3-inch rounds, using a floured cutter. Bake on the prepared pans for 15 to 18 minutes, until lightly golden around the edges.

Note: To vary the recipe, try adding 1 cup of miniature chocolate chips, raisins, nuts, or dried tart cherries (see Part V, "Sources") to the mix before adding the wet ingredients.

Pasta e Fagioli Mix

Italian comfort food made easy, this wholesome, multicolored mixture makes a wonderful meal with only the addition of a crusty loaf and maybe some mixed greens on the side. Your friends will appreciate having it in the pantry.

8 servings

½ cup each: dried cannellini or Great Northern beans, pinto beans, red beans, and cranberry or pink beans
¼ cup dried chopped onion
2 teaspoons dried minced garlic
1 bay leaf
1 teaspoon dried crumbled basil
½ teaspoon dried rosemary, crushed
1½ teaspoons salt
½ teaspoon pepper
1½ cups small bow ties, shells, macaroni, or other small pasta shapes (the multicolored varieties are good in this)

Sort through the beans, pulling out and discarding any shriveled specimens or dirt clumps. Mix them together, rinse in cold water, and spread out on paper towels to dry for several hours, or overnight if possible.

Combine the beans, onion, garlic, bay leaf, basil, rosemary, salt, and pepper. Package up the pasta separately.

To prepare: sauté 1 medium-sized chopped onion, 1 large chopped carrot, and 1 large, diced rib of celery in 2 tablespoons of olive oil until softened. Stir in the bean mixture, one 28-ounce can crushed tomatoes, and 2 quarts of chicken or vegetable stock, or water. Let the mixture boil gently for 10 minutes, then reduce the heat, cover the pan partially, and let it simmer until the beans are tender, 2 to 3 hours. Add the pasta and continue cooking until the pasta is al dente (usually 5 to 7 minutes, but be sure to check so it won't overcook). Serve immediately, passing these things as condiments: freshly ground imported Parmesan cheese, good olive oil (basil-flavored oil is great with this), and a pepper grinder.

Pork Chop Coating

The seasoning's all done when the cook has this convenience sitting on the pantry shelf. If you'd like a companion gift to go with this mix, consider one of the condiments in chapter 1, like maybe Apple-Onion Salsa, Pear Chutney, or Eggplant Pesto.

Enough to coat 8 chops

1	cup cornmeal
½	teaspoon paprika
1	teaspoon salt
½	teaspoon sugar
½	teaspoon powdered garlic
2	teaspoons dried chopped onion

Combine the ingredients, and place in a container with a tight-fitting lid.

To use, preheat the oven to 425 degrees. Brush the pork chops with a mixture of equal parts olive oil and Dijon mustard. Let sit for 30 minutes.

Allowing 2 teaspoons per chop, place the mix on a plate. Roll the chops in the mixture, coating all surfaces, then put them on a baking sheet and bake for 20 to 25 minutes—a touch longer if the chops are very thick, but take care not to overcook the meat.

Refried Bean Kit

Freshly cooked Mexican-style—and fat-free—beans have never been easier.

About 8 cups

4   cups dry pinto beans
½   cup dried chopped onion
¼   cup dried chopped green pepper
1   tablespoon granulated garlic
2   teaspoons dried red chili pepper
1   tablespoon salt
1   tablespoon ground cumin
Freshly ground pepper to taste

Sort through the beans, discarding any dirt clumps or shriveled beans. Rinse them, drain well, and spread on paper towels. Allow them to dry for at least 2 hours, preferably overnight. Mix with the remaining ingredients, and store at room temperature in an airtight container.

 To prepare the beans, shake the container to recombine the mix. Allowing about ½ cup mix per serving, place the beans in a medium saucepan and cover them with cold water. Bring to a boil and let bubble gently for 10 minutes, to release the toxins in the beans. Then reduce the heat, cover the pan partially, and cook at a gentle bubble for several hours, until very tender. Mash slightly and serve in a warm tortilla, use as a dip, or serve as a side dish all by itself.

Four-Bean Chili Mix

A kettle of hearty chili can chase away the chill on the most wicked of wintry days. What a nice gift to give!

6 to 8 servings

½   cup each: dried kidney, pinto, cranberry or pink, and Great Northern beans
2   tablespoons dried chopped onion
1   tablespoon dried chopped green pepper
½   teaspoon dried minced garlic
2   teaspoons chili powder
1   teaspoon ground cumin
¼   teaspoon cayenne pepper
1   teaspoon salt
½   teaspoon freshly ground pepper

Sort through the beans, discarding any shriveled ones or dirt clumps. Rinse them, then spread them out on paper towels to dry for at least 2 hours, preferably overnight.

Combine the beans, onion, green pepper, and garlic in a jar and mix well. Blend the chili powder, cumin, cayenne, salt, and pepper and package them separately.

To make the chili, cover the beans with cold water in a medium saucepan. Bring to a boil and let boil gently for 10 minutes. Turn off the heat, cover the pan, and let the beans sit 1 hour. Drain off the liquid, cover the beans with fresh water, bring to a boil, reduce the heat, and simmer until the beans are tender, 60 to 90 minutes. Drain the beans and set them aside.

While the beans are cooking in a large kettle, brown 1 pound beef chuck tender, cut into ½-inch cubes, in 1 tablespoon of hot olive oil in a large skillet. Add 1 medium-sized onion, chopped, 2 ribs of celery, sliced, and half of a medium-sized green bell pepper, chopped. Cook until the vegetables are softened. Add one 28-ounce can of tomatoes, cut into chunks, and the contents of the seasoning packet, and stir. Cover and simmer very gently for 60 to 90 minutes. If the chili seems to be getting too thick, add V-8 Juice as desired, to thin it out. Add the beans and simmer 30 minutes longer. Serve hot, garnished with shredded cheese, chopped onions, minced jalapeños, and/or sour cream, if desired.

Split Pea Soup Mix

On a blustery day, few foods can hit the spot quite like split pea soup. This mix makes it easy to put together.

6 to 8 servings

1	cup green split peas
1	cup yellow split peas
½	cup dried chopped onion
½	cup potato flakes
2	tablespoons dried parsley
1	bay leaf
	Salt and freshly ground pepper to taste

Sort through the split peas, discarding any dirt clumps or pebbles. Combine the peas in a strainer and run cold water over them to rinse them. Drain well, then spread the peas out on paper towels and let dry several hours or overnight.

Combine the peas with the remaining ingredients in a container with a tight-fitting lid. Store at room temperature.

To make the soup, combine the mix with 8 cups of water and a ham bone in a large kettle. Bring to a boil, reduce the heat, and simmer until the peas are tender, about 1½ to 2 hours. Remove the ham bone and bay leaf. Puree part or all of the mixture and return it to the pot. Mix in ¼ cup chopped fresh parsley and ¼ teaspoon of crumbled dried mint. Heat through and serve piping hot, garnished with chopped smoked ham and/or homemade croutons, if desired.

Tart Cherry Rice Pilaf Mix

This makes a flavorful side dish that goes together easily—nice to present with something that is going to be grilled and served with one of the condiments from chapter 1.

6 servings

1½ cups long-grain brown rice
¼ cup dried chopped onion
½ teaspoon salt
½ teaspoon allspice
½ teaspoon turmeric
¼ teaspoon curry powder
Freshly ground pepper to taste
½ cup chopped dried tart cherries (see note)
¼ cup slivered almonds, toasted

Combine the rice, onion, salt, spices, and pepper. Put in a decorative container and cover tightly.

Package the cherries and almonds in their own little respective packets and give with the rice mixture, perhaps all tied together with some raffia or ribbon.

Note: Dried tart cherries can be ordered via mail. See "Sources" (Part V).

To make the pilaf, first preheat the oven to 350 degrees. Heat 2 tablespoons olive oil in a large, oven-safe dish. Sauté the rice mixture gently in the oil until the rice is opaque, about 5 to 7 minutes. Add 3½ cups chicken or vegetable stock (preferably homemade), and bring to a rolling boil. Cover the dish, take it off the heat, and put it in the preheated oven. Bake for 60 to 75 minutes, until the rice is done. Stir in the cherries, replace the lid, turn the oven off, and let the pilaf sit in there about 5 minutes. Sprinkle almonds over the top and serve.

Chocolate Almond Pie Mix

For those who adore the combination of chocolate, coconut, and almonds, this mix yields a quick-fix pie with a crumbly, flavorful crust, a silky chocolate filling, and a golden topping of toasted coconut. What's more, it makes a fairly low-fat dessert, as incredible indulgences go. To bake the pie, your recipient will need to add vanilla extract, so you might like to wrap a bottle of vanilla with the mix.

1 pie

1	cup unsweetened coconut (available in health food and bulk grocery stores)
¼	cup slivered blanched almonds
1	cup plain granola
2	tablespoons firmly packed brown sugar
¼	cup unsweetened cocoa powder
⅓	cup granulated sugar
3	tablespoons nonfat dry milk
¼	cup cornstarch
½	teaspoon salt

Place the coconut in a dry, heavy skillet of medium size (cast iron works perfectly) over medium heat and toast, stirring constantly, until the coconut is light golden brown. Dump it onto a plate to cool, and wipe out the skillet if necessary and place it back on the stove. Put the almonds in it and toast them, stirring constantly, until they are lightly browned. Spread them out on another plate and let them cool.

Combine the granola and brown sugar in a food processor with the cooled almonds. Process for several seconds without stopping, until the mixture has a crumb consistency. Transfer it to a tightly covered container.

In a small bowl, combine the cocoa powder, sugar, dry milk, cornstarch, and salt. Mix well. Store in an airtight container.

Give the granola crust mix, the cocoa filling mix, and the toasted coconut grouped together in their respective containers, and fasten onto them these instructions:

 To make the pie, first preheat the oven to 350 degrees.

Put the pie crust mix in a medium bowl, and drizzle 2 tablespoons melted butter over it. Toss until the mixture is combined, then press it into the bottom and up the sides of a 9-inch pie pan. Bake until it begins to color, about 8 to 10 minutes. Cool.

Put 2 cups skim milk into a medium saucepan, and heat it to just below the boiling point.

While the milk heats up, put the pie filling mix into a medium bowl, and add ¾ cup of cold skim milk to it. Stir until smooth. Pour the hot milk into the bowl, stirring briskly, then return the mixture to the saucepan. Heat, stirring constantly, until the mixture comes to a boil. Continue cooking and stirring for 1 minute longer. Take it off the heat, and let it cool for 10 minutes, stirring several times to keep a skin from forming on the surface. Stir in 1 teaspoon vanilla.

Pour the filling into the cooled crust, and scatter the toasted coconut evenly over the top. Chill for several hours before serving.

Triple Chocolate-Tart Cherry Cookie Mix

Decadent and out of the ordinary, these cookies are packed with luscious things. The mix is a deluxe and unusual gift.

6 dozen cookies

> 1½ cups unbleached all-purpose flour
> ⅔ cup unsweetened cocoa powder
> ½ teaspoon baking soda
> ½ teaspoon salt
> ¼ teaspoon baking powder
> ⅛ teaspoon nutmeg
> 2¼ cups rolled oats
> 1 cup unsweetened coconut
> 1 cup semisweet chocolate chips
> 1 cup white baking chips
> ½ cup chopped pecans
> 1 cup dried tart cherries, chopped (see note)

Combine the flour, cocoa powder, soda, salt, baking powder, and nutmeg and stir with a fork. Stir in the oats, coconut, chips, pecans, and cherries. Store the mix in an airtight container.

Note: Dried tart cherries can be ordered through the mail. See "Sources" (Part V).

To make 3 dozen cookies, first preheat the oven to 350 degrees. Measure out half of the mix and set it aside.

In a large bowl, beat ½ cup vegetable shortening with ¾ cup firmly packed brown sugar until creamy. Beat in 1 egg, 2 teaspoons of milk, ¼ teaspoon of vanilla extract, and ¼ teaspoon of almond extract. Mix well. Add the mix and stir with a wooden spoon until thoroughly blended.

Roll the dough into 1-inch balls. Place on an ungreased cookie sheet and flatten to about 2 inches in diameter, leaving about an inch between the squashed balls of dough. Bake for 10 to 12 minutes. Cut up some brown paper grocery bags, and transfer the hot cookies to the brown paper to drain and cool. Store in an airtight container.

The Scoop on Cookie Mixes

The right tool makes the job, as they say, and there's a great little tool you can include in a gift of cookie mixes. It looks like an ice cream scoop, only smaller, and you use it to portion up perfect little balls of dough. You not only end up with uniformly sized cookies in record time, you also use your fingers less, so you walk away without having eaten a large portion of the dough—in case you're giving the mix to someone for whom that's a concern. To find miniature scoops, check in restaurant supply houses and other stores that sell cooks' gear.

Oatmeal Raisin Spice Cookie Mix

Chewy and packed with raisins, these wholesome cookies are the perfect after-school treat.

About 60 cookies

3   cups rolled oats
1   cup unbleached white flour
1   teaspoon salt
½   teaspoon baking soda
1   teaspoon cinnamon
¼   teaspoon cloves
Pinch of nutmeg
1   cup raisins

Combine all the ingredients, and store the mix in an airtight container.

〰️ To make the cookies, first preheat the oven to 350 degrees. Lightly grease a baking sheet.

In a large bowl, beat ¾ cup shortening, 1 cup firmly packed brown sugar, ½ cup granulated sugar, 1 egg, 2 tablespoons milk, and 1 teaspoon of vanilla until smooth. Stir in the mix and blend well. Drop the batter from a teaspoon onto the prepared baking sheet. Bake the cookies for 11 to 13 minutes. Transfer the hot cookies to cut-up brown paper grocery bags to drain and cool. Store in an airtight container.

Deluxe Chocolate Chip Cookie Mix

Everybody's favorite cookie, made easy with the help of a shortcut mix made and given by you. Believe it or not, the cookies will taste better if you use the fancy chocolate chips that don't skimp on natural ingredients; try a brand that uses real vanilla instead of vanillin. Your recipients will be glad you did.

6 dozen cookies

1¼ cups unbleached all-purpose flour
1   cup whole-wheat flour
1   teaspoon baking soda
½   teaspoon salt
1¾ cups semisweet chocolate chips
½   cup crushed toffee candy
1   cup chopped roasted, unsalted macadamia nuts

Combine everything in a large bowl, and then place the mix in an airtight container.

    To make 6 dozen cookies, first preheat the oven to 350 degrees.

Beat ⅔ cup granulated sugar, ⅔ cup firmly packed dark brown sugar, ½ cup softened unsalted butter, and ½ cup vegetable shortening until creamy. Add 2 large eggs, beating well after each, and 1 teaspoon vanilla extract. Stir in the mix and blend well.

Drop the batter from teaspoons onto ungreased baking sheets and bake for 11 to 13 minutes. Cut up brown paper grocery bags, and transfer the hot cookies to the brown paper to drain and cool.

Spanish-Style Rice Pilaf Mix

Between this convenient dish and the refried bean mix (see Index), Mexican dinners are easier than ever.

6 to 8 servings

2	cups long-grain white rice
½	cup dried chopped onion
¼	cup dried chopped green pepper
1	tablespoon dried minced garlic
2	teaspoons chili powder
1	teaspoon ground cumin
1	teaspoon salt
½	teaspoon freshly ground pepper

Mix the rice, onion, green pepper, and garlic in a jar until uniformly blended. Combine the chili powder, cumin, salt, and pepper and package the spices separately.

To prepare four servings, sauté 1 cup of the rice mixture slowly in 1 tablespoon of oil or butter until the rice becomes opaque. Stir in half of the seasoning packet, 1 cup (half of a 16-ounce can) of canned diced tomatoes with their liquid, and 1½ cups water. Bring to a boil, reduce the heat, cover, and simmer gently for 30 to 40 minutes, until the rice is tender.

Hot Cocoa Mix

Nothing chases away Jack Frost quite as pleasingly as a steaming mug of hot chocolate. This mix makes it easy to prepare.

About 14 servings

1½ cups unsweetened cocoa powder
2 cups sugar
4½ cups instant nonfat dry milk
¼ cup cornstarch
1 teaspoon cinnamon

Combine all the ingredients, using a sifter or whirling the mixture for a few seconds in the food processor to break up any lumps. Store in an airtight container.

To make one 8-ounce serving, put 2 or 3 tablespoons of the mix in a mug. Add ½ cup boiling water; stir until smooth. Add ½ cup more boiling water, stir well, and serve, topped with a marshmallow or a dollop of whipped cream, if desired.

EIGHT · *Try a Little Tenderness (Marinades)*

A savory solution to the problem of tough and/or flavor-destitute meats, marinades make a great gift for carnivores from all walks of life, be they grilling connoisseurs or roasting fans. The marinating principle—coaxing the meat into tenderizing a bit with the use of a judiciously administered and well-balanced acid of some sort—virtually guarantees improvement in both texture and flavor for any meat, fish, or fowl. That's a nice present to give.

Apple-Rosemary Marinade
(for pork or poultry)

Pork chops or roasts can do well with a soaking in this sweet-savory mixture.

1¼ cups

½   **cup vegetable oil**
¼   **cup cider vinegar**
½   **cup applesauce**
1   **medium-sized onion, sliced**
1   **teaspoon rosemary**
Salt and freshly ground pepper to taste

Combine everything and place in a covered jar. Chill.

Garlic-Dijon Marinade
(for chicken)

Marinades for poultry generally call for less vinegar and other acetic components, because the tender meat can be "cooked" if there's too much acid. That's also the reason that poultry needs less marinating time than red meats.

1 cup

¾   **cup olive oil**
2   **tablespoons Dijon mustard**
1   **tablespoon freshly squeezed lemon juice**
1   **tablespoon chopped fresh oregano (or 1 teaspoon dried)**
1   **or 2 cloves garlic, minced**
Salt and freshly ground pepper to taste

Mix everything together and store, covered, in the refrigerator.

Citrus Marinade
(for chicken and seafood)

Citrus fruits are a natural choice for marinating lighter meats. Do remind your recipient, though, that chicken and fish should be marinated for less time than beef or pork—generally no longer than an hour.

1³/₄ cups

1	**cup orange juice**
¼	**cup light olive oil**
2	**tablespoons dry sherry**
2	**tablespoons grapefruit juice**
1	**tablespoon each: freshly squeezed lemon juice, Dijon mustard, honey**
2	**teaspoons grated onion**
1	**clove garlic, minced**
½	**teaspoon paprika**
½	**teaspoon grated orange peel**
	Salt and freshly ground pepper to taste

Mix everything together thoroughly in a screw-top jar.

NINE ▪ *The Nursery Set*

Anyone who's ever had little mouths to feed can tell you that it's nice to have choices. Unfortunately, when it comes to top-of-the-line baby food, the pickings are slim. Making homemade baby goo is soul-satisfying work, to be sure, but it's tedious and time-consuming, and few new parents have great quantities of spare time on their hands. Fortunately, you have a gift for delicious gifts, and you can come to the rescue. That little bundle of joy need no longer suffer through a diet that highlights strained green beans and pureed prunes. Everybody deserves a treat from time to time, including the baby.

Truth in Labeling

It's never a bad idea to list the contents of a food you make to give away, but this is particularly wise when giving baby foods. To do it properly, you need to itemize the ingredients you use in order of their quantity, with the most plentiful component given first. With the ingredients on the package, a parent can give a quick glance to make sure that none of the things in the food are items to which the baby might have an allergy or is not yet ready to eat.

Basic Applesauce

The quintessential baby food, applesauce is both wholesome and easy to make, particularly if you have a hand-crank food mill among your cooking equipment. All it takes is some apples, a paring knife, and a big kettle. My mom taught me how to do this one cool autumn day a few years back. If your mom's not around, you can learn it from me instead.

Start with firm, ripe apples (oh, OK, you can use a few less-than-freshly-picked ones if you like—applesauce is forgiving stuff). Organic apples are good to use if you can find them. Don't use Red or Golden Delicious apples, organic or not—they're not designed for sauce. Cut out any bruises, then cut the apples lengthwise into quarters. Cut out the seeds if you have time; otherwise just drop the chunked apples, peels still on, into a kettle. If you don't have a food mill, peel and core the apples, then quarter them. Add a couple tablespoons of water, to prevent scorching, cover the kettle, and set it on the stove on medium heat. When the apples start to cook, reduce the heat to medium-low and let them cook, stirring occasionally, until very tender. This will take somewhere from 30 to 60 minutes. Keep an eye on them to make sure they don't burn onto the bottom of the kettle.

When the apples are finished cooking, transfer them to the food mill and process them to extract the seeds and skins. (If you peeled and cored them before cooking, simply mash them by hand or in a food processor.) Transfer the sauce to jars, cover tightly, and refrigerate, or put the sauce into freshly sterilized jars and seal them according to the general canning instructions given in Part IV ("Basics"), processing for 15 minutes if the jars are pint-sized or 20 minutes if they are quart jars.

Variations: Of course, you can add a sweetener to applesauce if you like. Brown sugar and honey both work well, added to taste, but be sure to use only brown sugar if the sauce is going to be eaten by an infant, because it is believed that honey poses a slight botulism risk for babies under a year old. I don't usually add any sweetening to applesauce, believing that it amounts to gilding the lily. But you should use your own taste or the preferences of the baby's parents as a guide.

For fruit-enhanced applesauce, add the fruits, usually using about half as much as the amount of apples you're cooking, after the mixture has started to simmer. Apricots, peaches, plums, and pears can be put in shortly after cooking begins, while berries will need less cooking time (bear in mind, though, that parents usually are advised to wait until after the baby is a year old before introducing berries into the diet, to minimize the risk of developing allergies). When all the fruits are tender, mill or puree the mixture.

For additional flavor enhancement, you can add spices such as cinnamon, cloves, ginger, nutmeg, and/or allspice. A dash of rum also deepens the flavor of applesauce but probably isn't appropriate for the baby.

Fruit-Flavored Zwieback

We adults can only imagine how it must feel to have teeth cutting through tender gums. It would be enough to make anybody cranky. With these tasty toast fingers, teething might be just a bit less difficult. Giving them to your favorite tooth sprouter might make you a true hero in that baby's house.

¼ cup brown sugar
⅓ cup vegetable oil
2 eggs
1 cup mashed fruit (bananas, cooked apples, peaches, and/or pears)
2 teaspoons soy flour (see note below)
2 teaspoons nonfat dry milk
1 tablespoon wheat germ
1½ cups flour (white and/or whole wheat)
1 teaspoon baking powder
½ teaspoon baking soda

Preheat the oven to 350 degrees. Oil an 8-inch square pan.

Mix the sugar and oil; beat in the eggs, then the fruit. Mix the dry ingredients together and fold them into the fruit mixture, stirring only until everything is blended. Turn the batter into the prepared pan, spreading it with a rubber spatula to an even thickness. Bake for an hour, until firmly set. Take out the bread and reduce the oven to 200 degrees.

Cool the bread in the pan, then remove it and cut the square in half. Slice each half crosswise into ½- to ¾-inch-thick fingers. Spread the pieces out on a cookie sheet, cut surfaces up, and bake them at 200 degrees for 2 hours or longer, until they are dry and crunchy. Store the biscuits in an airtight container.

Note: Soy flour, a powerhouse source of protein, can be found in health food stores.

Peanut Butter Pancakes

Peanut butter is a bit too sticky for many babies to handle, so parents usually are urged to avoid giving it to the baby. But these pancakes give a way for self-feeding babies, who are older than about a year, to enjoy the flavor of peanut butter in a much neater, less sticks-to-the-roof-of-the-mouth way.

2   eggs, beaten
¼   cup honey
½   teaspoon vanilla extract
½   cup smooth peanut butter
¾   cup milk
1   cup whole-wheat flour
¼   cup nonfat dry milk
½   teaspoon salt
2   teaspoons baking powder

Beat the eggs, honey, vanilla, and peanut butter together until smooth. Add the ¾ cup milk and mix well.

Combine the flour, dry milk, salt, and baking powder. Stir into the milk mixture and blend well.

Fry the batter in 3- to 4-inch rounds on a lightly oiled griddle until golden brown on both sides.

For gift giving, wrap the pancakes, in stacks of two or three, securely in plastic wrap. If it's going to be more than a couple of hours before you present the pancakes, store them, wrapped, in the refrigerator.

PART III

PACKAGE DEALS:
PULLING IT ALL TOGETHER

One of the best things about homemade food gifts is the way you can assemble them in configurations specifically suited for the occasion that has prompted their being given. Sometimes this calls for a present that is 100 percent homemade, right down to the gift tags. Other times you might opt to buy part of the present—some pure maple syrup to go with a pancake mix; a set of crystal pony glasses to go with a bottle of coffee liqueur; a box of nice steaks to go with a jar of relish or salsa; a pasta fork to tie onto a bundle of homemade linguine.

Of course the best way to assemble a collection of food gifts is to use your own imagination, your familiarity with the tastes of the person to whom you're giving the goodies, and the finest resources available to you. But to get you started, here are some suggestions:

- **Cookie Monster Special**   Find a really great cookie jar, if your gift budget allows it, or fashion a homemade box as simple as paper- or fabric-covered cardboard, and pack in it one of each of the three cookie mixes from chapter 7: Triple Chocolate-Tart Cherry, Deluxe Chocolate Chip, and Oatmeal Raisin Spice.

- **Pasta 'n' Sauce**   Churn out a couple of flavors of pasta, maybe cutting one batch as linguine and the other as fettucine, and pack them in a cloth-lined basket with a jar of Marinara Sauce, a jar of Alfredo Sauce, a bottle of basil oil, and a tub of pesto. If you include a chunk of imported Parmesan cheese, a crusty loaf of bread, and a bottle of nice wine, they'll be wanting for nothing more.

- **You Big Baby**   Here's a baby gift for the no-longer-newborn. Deliver an array of toothsome treats for the neophyte eater, including chapter 9's Basic Applesauce (plain or blended with other fruits), Fruit-flavored Zwieback, and Peanut Butter Pancakes, and one of the granolas from chapter 4—made into baby muesli by omitting the nuts and processing it briefly in a food processor to reduce its chunkiness. Try packing the gifts in a doll bassinet or a tiny wagon, maybe tucking in a little toy as a special bonus.
- **The Drawing Room Special**   As in, "Shall we repair to the drawing room for cigars and brandy?" Perhaps you can use an elegant serving tray for a presentation vessel. Mix a few of the after-dinner drinks from chapter 6—Irish Cream, Coffee Liqueur, Mint Liqueur, and Plum Brandy—and give along with wishes for a satisfying dinner with stimulating conversationalists, and perhaps a couple of nice snifters or other after-dinner glassware. Cigars are optional.
- **Welcome to the Neighborhood**   Anyone who's ever pulled up stakes and tackled that daunting occasion known as Moving Day can attest that it takes time to settle into new surroundings. To make it easier for the folks who just put the roof of a nearby house over their heads, you might take over something friendly, freshly made, and ready to enjoy, such as "Nibblings" (chapter 4) or any of the juice mixes in chapter 6. The gift also might include a batch of Buttermilk Baking Mix and the cookbooklet that accompanies it, for the several weeks of somewhat frantic meals that are sure to follow the big moving day. Any of the other mixes likely would be put to good use, too. Don't forget to tuck into the basket your phone number and maybe a few fresh flowers, to make the place seem a little more homey.

- **Deluxe Campers' Provisions** For family or friends who are setting off to the wilderness—or as a surprise for your own camping companions—combine gift foods that will produce unparalleled outdoor meals: some canned Barbecue Sauce (chapter 1); Buttermilk Baking Mix, Hot Cocoa Mix, and a Refried Bean Kit (chapter 7); and Stovetop or Baked Granola (chapter 4), all of which pack well and will satisfy the appetite whetted by living in wide open spaces.

- **Breakfast Time** A selection of first-thing-in-the-morning goodies makes a nice gift, especially for someone with a new job that requires early rising and needs incentive, or for the new retiree who suddenly has mornings to linger over. Try some Whole-Grain Pancake Mix and Ginger Muffin Mix from chapter 7 and a jar of one of the granolas from chapter 4. You might throw in a couple of grapefruits and a sack of exotic coffee beans to round out the eye-opening feast.

- **The Chill Chaser** A heartwarming gift might include Pasta e Fagioli Mix, Four-Bean Chili Mix, and Split Pea Soup Mix (all chapter 7). Packed into a generously proportioned soup tureen or with a couple of deep mugs, they would make a cherished gift that would be remembered fondly during the blustery months of winter.

- **Newlywed Basket** The just-married can, and often do, live on love alone, but a little romantic picnic never hurt anybody. Chapter 1 is full of tasty ideas, such as Gramma's Chicken Liver Pâté, Poor Man's Boursin, the chutneys, maybe some store-bought chocolates, a fresh and crusty loaf of bread from a good bakery, and a nice bottle of wine would make a nice package. Don't forget the red-checked cloth.

- **Road Trip Survival Kit** Snacks that aren't too messy are a good choice for long car rides, and if they're particularly tasty, they can really help break the monotony. For a good bon voyage collection, see chapter 4, "Nibblings," and pack Pesto Pecans, Gramma's Herb Toast, White Chocolate Trail Mix, and Maplecorn. If you're presenting it right at departure time, you can throw in a few bottles of chilled water or juice and some freshly cut vegetables and pieces of fruit, and there might not have to be any heartburn-inducing fast-food stops.

- **Tea Time**   A well-made teapot should be part of every kitchen. Pack it in a basket lined with a nice flowery cloth napkin, along with a couple of flavors of herb tea, a good tea ball, and some Scone Mix or Ginger Muffin Mix (chapter 7). Or both.
- **Tex-Mex Dinner Kit**   Into a basket put some Green Chile Salsa (chapter 1); a pretty bottle of Mexican-Style Oil (chapter 3); a jar of Spanish-Style Rice Pilaf Mix and a Refried Bean Kit (chapter 7); some fresh tortillas; and maybe a hunk of cheese. A full-fledged Mexican feast is just a few easy steps away.
- **Muffin Mania**   Along with maybe a nice muffin pan, pack a few of the muffin mixes that appear in chapter 7, or perhaps some Buttermilk Baking Mix, also in that chapter. Some stores sell cupcake papers with droll designs on them, and those are a fun thing to include in a muffin basket, too.
- **Dorm Food Antidote**   A collegiate care package full of homemade goodies can ease pangs of homesickness and cafeteria blues by filling the belly with comforting flavors. If the scholar hasn't a hot plate or other heating appliance on hand, you might include one with an assortment of foods from chapters 1, 4, and 7, such as Gramma's Herb Toast, Green Chile Salsa and a bag of good tortilla chips, perhaps a soup or chili mix, some granola, Hot Cocoa Mix, and maybe some Maplecorn or Pesto Pecans. There, now, midterms and term papers don't seem so awful, do they?

- **Pizza Kit**   Try giving a ready-made crust, or a boxed crust mix, along with a jar of Marinara Sauce (chapter 1), a small collection of fresh vegetables for toppings (onion, peppers, mushrooms, and broccoli, perhaps), maybe a little crock of one of the pestos in chapter 1, and a chunk of nice mozzarella cheese.
- **Grillers' Assortment**   For the patio gourmet, pack up a variety of marinades and condiments that are well suited to food cooked over the open flame: perhaps a salsa, a chutney, a relish, and one of the butters. Stick a grilling gadget or two in among the goodies and arrange everything on a nice serving platter. Wrap the whole collection in a big sheet of cellophane and top it off with a bodacious bow.
- **A Basket of Goodwill**   Some gifts bring special symbolism. Sage, believed from ages past to be a source of health and salvation, can be given in the form of the fragrant green Sage Pesto sauce. To go with it, some noodles—associated by the Chinese with longevity—would be nice. Include in the basket a crusty loaf of bread—the staff of life, you know—and perhaps a bottle of wine, to nourish the soul. A scattering of foil-wrapped chocolate coins, given in the Orient to bring luck, would finish off a most symbolic grouping of gifts. For the pesto and pasta, see chapters 1 and 5, respectively.
- **Cabin Fever First Aid Kit**   Some eye-opening comfort foods can help make the late-winter blues seem a little less severe. A variety of the chapter 7 mixes—Pasta e Fagioli, Four-Bean Chili, Scone and Ginger Muffin mixes, for example—can give the listless sun worshiper something to do in those hardest, final few weeks of winter weather. Throw in a good board game or a can't-put-it-down bestseller, and the time will pass even more quickly.

- **The Make-Up-Your-Own Gift Basket**   This one is up to you. Ponder the needs and pleasures of your family and friends, scan the recipes for perfect combinations, look around for just the right containers and trimmings, and put together a personally designed package certain to be much appreciated and enjoyed.

PART IV

❖❖❖❖❖❖❖❖❖❖❖❖❖❖❖❖❖❖❖❖❖❖❖❖

BASICS: A FIRM FOUNDATION

Any good workshop needs to be equipped with the right tools. Similarly, a cook who wants to take on any challenge thrown his or her way needs to be armed with all the skills that might be called into play. One of these techniques, hot-water bath canning, is mentioned in these pages. It's a valuable bit of culinary capability to have in one's repertoire, so a general description of the process is given here.

A well-prepared cook also wants to have on hand all of the supplies that will be needed to get the job done. So also appearing in this section is a list of basic grocery items that are good to keep on hand, plus a listing of things that can be substituted for ingredients that are in short supply or nowhere to be found. And because the "net" quantities given on packages in the supermarket don't always seem to translate directly to the unit of measurement required in a recipe, a conversion chart also is included here.

Hot-Water Bath Canning

High-acid foods, including fruits, tomatoes, and pickled vegetables, are best preserved by submerging sealed jars in a covered kettle of boiling water. Of the foods included in this book, the chutneys, the barbecue sauce, and the applesauce are most suitable for water-bath canning.

The principle is simple: hot, freshly cooked food is packed into hot, freshly sterilized glass containers, sealed, and heated to a sufficient temperature to kill any organisms that may remain in the food. The resultant vacuum-sealed container will keep the food fresh and safe to eat without refrigeration for quite a while—some people will tell you forever, but generally the nutritional content and the quality of flavor will decline as time goes on. Most home-canned foods should be stored in a relatively cool spot and eaten up within 12 months.

A few pieces of equipment are good to have on hand for canning. The process can be done without them, but they are worthwhile tools to invest in if you expect to can food more than once or twice. Most of them can be found in a well-stocked hardware store.

First of all, a large kettle is critical. It needs to be deep enough so that the water can come up to about an inch above the tops of the jars, and there will still be enough space (a couple of inches at least) for the water to boil. It should have a snug-fitting lid. To ease the task of putting the jars into the kettle full of boiling water and taking them out again, you should have a rack made for this purpose. A jar funnel—the kind with a lower opening about two inches across—is handy to have, so things don't get too messy when you're spooning the food into the jars, and a pair of jar tongs, designed to grab the jar by its rim, also is a good tool. A couple of wire racks are useful for holding the jars while they cool, so the air can circulate freely around the hot glass.

Now you're ready to start. The most important rule-of-thumb in home canning is cleanliness. Most of us have heard cases of families being stricken with botulism after eating improperly home-canned goods. Careful preparation and fastidious attention to matters of sanitation can prevent this.

Be sure your hands, all working surfaces, utensils, cooking vessels, and containers are as free of germs as you can make them. (Yes, this means you have to scrub the sink if you're going to wash fruit or vegetables in it.)

Take care to choose good canning jars, and always use new rubber-rimmed lids that have a dimple in the middle—this will help you identify a good seal when you're finished. If the jars aren't brand-new, check them over carefully to be sure there are no chips or cracks.

The jars usually can be sterilized while your food is cooking. After you have washed the jars and lids in hot, soapy water, immerse them in a kettle of boiling water (I usually use the canning kettle for this), and boil them for at least 10 minutes. Put the jars and rings into a separate saucepan, cover them with almost-boiling water, and keep them over low heat until you're ready to use them.

When the food is finished cooking, take the jars out of the kettle and put them upside-down on clean linen towels. Using a ladle and a jar funnel if you have one, fill each jar to within about ½ inch of the rim of the jar. Using a towel dipped into hot water and wrung out, carefully wipe any drips of food off the lip of the jar. Drain the jar lids and rings, and place a two-piece top onto each jar. Tighten the lid only lightly; do not screw it down all the way.

Using jar tongs if you have them, lower the jars into the boiling water. In the absence of tongs, you can load the jars into the rack first and then lower the whole thing carefully into the kettle. Be sure the jars are not touching one another, because this can lead to breakage.

Add or remove water, if necessary, to bring the level to one inch above the jar tops (it's a good idea to have a teakettle of boiling water ready for this, just in case). Cover the kettle and begin timing. When the specified period is up, remove the jars and set them on racks covered with clean linen towels, leaving space between them. As they cool, you might hear them "pop" as the seal is formed. Wait until they are completely cooled to test for a seal: Press each lid in its center. If it pops up and down, refrigerate the jar right away and eat up the food soon. If the middle of the jar stays down, label it, specifying the contents and date, and store it in a cool place.

There! Wasn't that easy?

The Well-Stocked Pantry

Few of us enjoy running out to the grocery store for one item. Yet without a kitchen stocked with the right collection of basic staples, this can happen too easily—and just when you were all set to get started cooking! So, as a sort of checklist, here is a collection of items that is good to keep on hand. If you have the luxury of freezer space, consider picking up some of the items listed here that you don't normally keep around. Things that freeze well include bran, most flours, butter, coconut, coffee, cornmeal, dry mustard, most herbs and spices, margarine, powdered milk, nuts, oats, tapioca, and yeast.

Baking powder

Baking soda

Beans (canned): kidney, garbanzos

Beans (dry): Great Northern or navy, kidney, lentils, split peas, black turtle, black-eyed peas, pinto

Bouillon cubes or powder—chicken, beef, and vegetable (for emergency use, when homemade and canned versions are unavailable)

Bran—wheat and/or oat

Butter—unsalted and regular varieties

Canned fruits—unsweetened, a variety

Catsup

Chiles—mild green chiles, jalapeños, and chitpotle peppers in cans; dried pasada and ancho peppers

Clams (canned)

Chocolate: unsweetened, semisweet, or bittersweet baking chocolate and semisweet chips

Cocoa powder (unsweetened)

Coconut, shredded (unsweetened)

Coffee—beans and instant powdered

Cornmeal

Cornstarch

Crackers—plain, for spreads

Cream of tartar

Dried fruits—raisins, currants, cherries

Extracts—vanilla (make it a good one), almond, lemon

Flour—unbleached all-purpose, whole-wheat, cake or pastry, semolina (for pasta), rye

Frozen breadstuffs: puff pastry, eggroll and/or wonton skins, English muffins

Frozen fruits: berries, peaches

Gelatin (unflavored)

Herbs and spices—replace at least once every couple of years

Honey

Horseradish

Hot pepper sauce

Juices (bottled and/or frozen)—lemonade, orange, apple

Liqueurs—Grand Marnier, cognac, Amaretto

Margarine—stick type, corn oil-based

Milk—evaporated, sweetened condensed, nonfat dry, powdered buttermilk

Molasses

Mushrooms (dried)—shiitake, porcini

Mustard—Dijon, prepared yellow, honey

Nuts—pecans, walnuts, almonds (whole raw and blanched, slivered, and sliced varieties), pine nuts

Oats—old-fashioned and quick-cooking

Oils—olive, canola, safflower or sunflower, corn, sesame, Asian chili oil

Pasta—a variety of dried shapes, including spaghetti or linguine; large shells or manicotti, penne, macaroni, or another form of tubular shaped noodle; plus frozen tortellini and ravioli

Peanut butter

Pesto (frozen)

Pickles—dill, sweet relish

Preserves—fruit mixtures as spreads, plus currant jelly or apricot jam, for glazes

Potatoes—russet and redskin

Rice—long-grain white, brown, wild, converted

Salsa—mild and hot

Soy sauce

Stocks (frozen or canned)—chicken, beef, fish, vegetable

Sun-dried tomatoes (canned in oil)

Sugar—granulated, brown, and powdered types; "raw" (turbinado) sugar also is good to have on hand

Syrups—pure maple, light, and dark corn

Tapioca—pearl and quick-cooking types

Tea—black and herbal varieties

Tomatoes (canned)—whole, diced, paste, pureed

Tuna (water-packed)

Vanilla beans (1 or 2 are enough)

Vinegars—cider, red wine, white wine, balsamic, rice

Wines—dry red, dry white, dry sherry, vermouth, port

Worcestershire sauce

Yeast—active dry and brewer's

Making Do: Substitutions Allowed

Then again, sometimes you don't have to run out to the store for just one item. Given here are some things that are allowed to stand in for an ingredient you might be both needing and lacking. Sometimes you'll need to make the effort to use the real McCoy in a recipe, but it isn't always critical. Use your discretion.

Arrowroot (as a thickener)—for each teaspoon, use 1 teaspoon flour or 1½ teaspoons cornstarch

Baking powder—for each teaspoon, use ¼ teaspoon baking soda plus ½ teaspoon cream of tartar

Butter—margarine or, if melted, just over half as much strained bacon fat or ⅞ as much vegetable oil can be substituted

Buttermilk—plain yogurt or, for each cup, use 1 tablespoon vinegar or lemon juice plus enough milk to make a cup

Chocolate, unsweetened—for each ounce, use 3 tablespoons unsweetened cocoa powder plus 1 tablespoon vegetable oil or melted shortening

Chocolate, semisweet—for each ounce, substitute 1½ teaspoons unsweetened cocoa powder plus 2 tablespoons sugar and 2 table-spoons vegetable oil or melted shortening

Cocoa—for each ¼ cup, substitute 1 ounce unsweetened chocolate and omit 1½ teaspoons of the fat

Cracker crumbs—for each ¾ cup crumbs needed, substitute 1 cup bread crumbs

Cream, light (or half-and-half)—for each cup, use 1½ tablespoons melted butter plus 7 ounces (¾ cup plus 2 tablespoons) milk

Cream, heavy (or whipping cream)—for each cup, use ⅓ cup melted butter plus ¾ cup milk, but don't try to whip it

Egg yolks (for thickening)—you may use one whole egg for each 2 yolks called for

Flour, cake—for each cup (sifted), substitute ⅞ cup (¾ cup plus 2 tablespoons) sifted all-purpose flour

Flour, all-purpose white (for baking)—for each cup, substitute 1 cup cake flour plus 2 tablespoons all-purpose flour, ⅓ cup cornmeal plus ⅔ cup all-purpose flour, ½ cup bran plus ½ cup all-purpose flour, ½ cup rice flour plus ½ cup all-purpose flour, ½ cup rye flour plus ½ cup all-purpose flour, ¼ cup soy flour plus ¾ cup all-purpose flour, or ¾ cup whole-wheat flour plus ¼ cup all-purpose flour

Flour (as a thickener)—for each tablespoon needed, use 1½ teaspoons cornstarch, potato starch, rice starch, or arrowroot, or 1 tablespoon quick-cooking tapioca

Garlic, minced—for each clove, substitute ⅛ teaspoon garlic powder or granulated garlic

Herbs, fresh—generally use ⅓ as much dried herb in place of the fresh quantity specified

Honey—for each cup, use 1¼ cups sugar plus ¼ cup liquid

Horseradish, fresh—for each tablespoon, substitute 2 tablespoons bottled

Lard—vegetable shortening or bacon fat

Lemon juice—for each teaspoon, substitute ½ teaspoon vinegar (plain or compatibly flavored)

Lemon rind, grated—for each teaspoon, substitute ½ teaspoon lemon extract

Liquor (rum, bourbon, or whiskey)—for each ½ cup, substitute ¼ cup unsweetened fruit juice or broth

Maple sugar—granulated sugar

Maple syrup—honey, molasses, or, for each cup, 1⅓ cups granulated or packed brown sugar

Milk, whole—for each cup, substitute ½ cup evaporated milk plus ½ cup water, ¼ cup nonfat dry milk powder plus ⅞ cup water and 2 teaspoons melted butter or margarine, 1 cup skim milk plus 2 teaspoons whipping cream or melted butter or margarine, or 1 cup soy milk

Milk, lowfat or skim—for each cup, use ⅓ cup nonfat dry milk powder plus ⅞ cup water

Molasses—honey or maple syrup

Mushrooms, canned—for each 6-ounce can, drained, substitute about 1 cup sliced, cooked fresh mushrooms

Mushrooms, dried—for each ounce, substitute about ⅓ pound fresh mushrooms

Mustard, dry—for each teaspoon, use 1 tablespoon prepared mustard

Onion—for 1 small, chopped onion, substitute 1 teaspoon onion powder or 1 tablespoon dried minced onion

Sugar, granulated—brown sugar, packed, or, for each cup, substitute 1¾ cups sifted powdered sugar

Tapioca, quick-cooking—replace with twice as much regular pearl tapioca

Tomato juice—for each cup, substitute ½ cup tomato sauce plus ½ cup water

Tomato sauce—for 2 cups, use one 6-ounce can (¾ cup) tomato paste and 1 cup water

Sour cream—for each cup, substitute ⅓ cup butter plus ¾ cup buttermilk or yogurt

Wine—flavored vinegars can take the place of wine or, for white wine, you can substitute apple or white grape juice in an equal quantity; for red, use unsweetened purple grape juice. Reduce sugar if necessary to balance the sweetness of the juice.

Convertibles: Interpreting Quantities

When it comes to cooking, most of us are unilingual. Anyone who's ever done much traveling can tell you it's sometimes difficult to hop from one currency to another, from one language to a much different one, pretty much from any unit of measure to any other system. When we cook, we often need to translate from ounces to cups or kilograms, to halve or triple or divide a recipe by thirds. So given here are a few equivalents for units that might one day cross your culinary path.

Volume equivalents (quantities apply to both liquid and dry ingredients unless specified otherwise):

A pinch = less than ⅛ teaspoon (dry)

A dash = less than ¼ teaspoon (liquid)

1 teaspoon = about 60 drops (liquid) or ⅓ tablespoon

½ tablespoon = 1½ teaspoons

1 tablespoon = 3 teaspoons or ½ fluid ounce
1 fluid ounce = 2 tablespoons
¼ cup = 4 tablespoons or 2 ounces (liquid)
⅓ cup = 5 tablespoons plus 1 teaspoon
⅜ cup = ¼ cup plus 2 tablespoons
½ cup = 8 tablespoons or 4 ounces (liquid)
⅝ cup = ½ cup plus 2 tablespoons
⅔ cup = ½ cup plus 2 tablespoons plus 2 teaspoons
¾ cup = 12 tablespoons or 6 ounces (liquid)
⅞ cup = ¾ cup plus 2 tablespoons
1 cup = ½ pint or 8 ounces
1 pint = 2 cups or ½ quart
1 quart = 4 cups or 2 pints or 32 ounces (liquid)
1 gallon = 4 quarts or 128 ounces (liquid)
1 peck = 16 pints (dry)
1 bushel = 4 pecks or 64 pints (dry)

Metric conversions:
1 centimeter = 0.394 inch
1 inch = 2.54 centimeters
1 meter = 39.37 inches
1 liter = 33.8 ounces
1 ounce = 28.3 grams

Temperature conversions:

−10 degrees Fahrenheit = −23.3 degrees Celsius (freezer storage temperature)

0 degrees F = −17.7 degrees C

32 degrees F = 0 degrees C (freezing point for water)

50 degrees F = 10 degrees C

68 degrees F = 20 degrees C (room temperature)

100 degrees F = 37.7 degrees C

150 degrees F = 65.5 degrees C

205 degrees F = 96.1 degrees C (simmering temperature for water)

212 degrees F = 100 degrees C (boiling point for water)

300 degrees F = 148.8 degrees C (slow oven)

325 degrees F = 162.8 degrees C

350 degrees F = 177 degrees C (normal baking temperature)

375 degrees F = 190.5 degrees C

400 degrees F = 204.4 degrees C (hot oven)

425 degrees F = 218.3 degrees C

450 degrees F = 232 degrees C

475 degrees F = 246.1 degrees C

500 degrees F = 260 degrees C (broiling)

PART V

SOURCES

Food

SPECIAL
59¢ lb.

In accumulating the raw materials needed to put together some of the treats described in the preceding recipes, you might be called on to look beyond the grocer's shelves. Most of the goods listed in this book can be found at the corner market, but not all of them. Sometimes you'll need to head for specialty stores or other specialized merchants to find what you need. Do remember that all the legwork that goes into this is, after all, a labor of love. Otherwise you'd be perfectly content to let the corner gourmet store pack up a basket for you.

In this section are given some ideas for places to go when the supermarket is unable to furnish the supplies you need.

For fresh foods, there are farmers' markets, where often you can buy large quantities of just-picked fruits, vegetables, herbs, syrup, and honey, and store them until needed. Often it makes sense to stock up: berries, peaches, many-colored bell peppers, and fresh plum tomatoes are just a few of the items that freeze obligingly, waiting to be plucked out months later, when their most attractive counterpart in your supermarket is a far inferior specimen.

If you live near a big city, be sure to check local produce stores during the off season; perhaps they buy their goods fresh every day from a metropolitan supplier. I once got a gorgeous bundle of basil in the middle of February this way. It wasn't cheap, but it was the absolute dead of winter, I had to have some homemade pesto, and money was no object.

As for the dry goods, a certain portion of them probably sit on your pantry shelf all the time. Do check to make sure they haven't been sitting there too long; dried herbs and spices last a long time, but not forever. A good whiff should tell you whether there's much flavor left in the jar, let alone a quarter-teaspoon.

If you are having trouble locating a dry goods item, consider trying bulk grocery stores (the Chicago area has a chain of stores known as the Home Economist, where all manner of unusual foods can be found in the exact quantity you need).

Last, but not least, are mail-order purveyors, who often stock fascinating collections of hard-to-find edible goods. Most of these people will happily send you a catalog just for the asking. This can amount to a convenient, headache-free way to shop for some of the less readily available ingredients found in a few of the recipes here. A few are listed below.

American Spoon Foods, Inc.
P.O. Box 566
Petoskey, MI 49770-0566
Phone: 616-347-9030/800-222-5886
Fax: 616-347-2512

Fruit preservation specialists, the people at American Spoon combine their inspired creativity with the raw goodness of locally derived ingredients to come up with a dazzling array of treats, from Red Haven Peach Preserves and Red Raspberry Butter to dried Michigan morel mushrooms and pickled snap peas. Among their most popular items are the dried tart Montmorency cherries, grown in northwestern Michigan, which they sell in packages ranging in sizes from 3 ounces to 1 pound.

Arctic Acres
Box 380
Greensboro, VT 05842
Phone: 800-544-5410
Pure Vermont grade A maple syrup is the specialty of this business, which offers its nectar in gallon-sized containers as well as smaller increments.

Chamomile Farms, Inc.
760 W. Hampshire Blvd.
Citrus Springs, FL 34434
Phone: 800-548-1592
This enterprise offers whole vanilla beans and extracts from Madagascar, maple syrup and related products, and a good sampling of culinary herbs and spices.

Community Kitchens
P.O. Box 2311 Dept. JG
Baton Rouge, LA 70821-2311
Phone: 800-535-9901
Fax: 800-321-7539
Pepper blends, olive oil, and balsamic vinegar are among the "fancy foods" described in the eye-pleasing catalog, titled *The Art of Food*, distributed by this bayou-accented company. Cooking equipment, kitchen gadgets, serving apparatuses, and assorted gift-appropriate items also are offered.

Fox Hill Farm
444 W. Michigan
P.O. Box 9
Parma, MI 49269
Phone: 517-531-3179

Basil experts of the highest order, the people at Fox Hill specialize in all kinds of growing and fresh-cut herbs, which they will ship gathered in bunches, wound into topiary, or assembled in pots in a variety of cooking collections. There's even a culinary herb basket, designed to hang in the kitchen, where the greens can be snipped as they are needed.

Frontier Cooperative Herbs
Herb and Spice Collection Division
P.O. Box 299
Norway, IA 52318
Phone: 800-786-1388

Herb and Spice Collection is the name of the retail branch of this savory enterprise, which does much of its business with natural food cooperatives and food buying clubs. Inventory offered through the retail catalog includes herbs, spices, teas, coffees, essential oils, certified organically grown herbs, Chinese herbs, spice blends, bulk products, powdered and dried vegetables, gelatin capsules, popcorn seasonings, Tao tea, Chinese herb tea, assorted extracts and natural flavorings, vegetable and cosmetic oils, fragrances, herb and spice accessories, coffee and tea accessories, and handcrafted pottery.

Le Jardin du Gourmet
P.O. Box 75
St. Johnsbury Center, VT 05863
Phone: 802-748-1446

A massive quantity of Dijon-style mustard—10 pounds, to be exact—is one of the entries on the product list for this seasoning specialty company. Herb plants, sets for growing members of the onion family (garlic, onions, shallots), and vinegars also are offered via mail.

Manganaro Foods
488 Ninth Ave.
New York, NY 10018
Phone: 212-563-5331/800-4-SALAMI (472-5264)

A good selection of oils, vinegars, and cheeses are included in the inventory of this 100-year-old, family-run business, which features imported Italian grocery items. Their catalog also offers a sumptuous array of sausages, pastas, and Italian-made sweets.

The Sandy Mush Herb Nursery
Rte. 2, Surrett Cove Rd.
Leicester, NC 28748-9622
Phone: 704-683-2014 (9 A.M. to 5 P.M., EST, Thursday, Friday, and
    Saturday only)

A long and impressive list of herbs, grasses, and perennial flowering plants is available from this nursery. They'll also plant for you an herb garden or collections of teas, bonsai plants, or flowering perennials. Table-sized trees, herb and flower seeds, herb-related books, and note cards can be purchased here too.

Taylor's Herb Garden
1535 Lone Oak Rd.
Vista, CA 92084
Phone: 619-727-3485
Fax: 619-727-0289
More than 170 varieties of seeds are sold by this business, in addition to nearly every live herb plant imaginable.

Watkins Inc.
150 Liberty St.
Winona, MN 55987-0570
Phone: 800-247-5907
Founded just after the end of the Civil War, Watkins specializes in spices, extracts, and flavorings that are sold by mail as well as through a network of 50,000 independent distributors. The 125-year-old company's line today includes an intriguing collection of spice blends in addition to sauces, grooming preparations, nutritional supplements, and assorted household products.

Well-Sweep Herb Farm
317 Mount Bethel Rd.
Port Murray, NJ 07865
Phone: 908-852-5390
A live herb plant can make a wonderful companion to many gifts of food. For pure grow-your-own herb pleasures, this purveyor of green things is difficult to outdo. Their no-nonsense catalog offers around 1,400 varieties of live plants, and several dozen kinds of herb seeds, too, if you prefer to grow your own herbs from scratch.

Williams-Sonoma
P.O. Box 7456
San Francisco, CA 94120-7456
Phone: 800-541-2233
Vinegars, oils, tomato paste in a tube, and assorted spices are among the foods that appear in this beautiful periodic *Catalog for Cooks.*

Vessels

Several nationally franchised stores carry great collections of attractive possibilities for containers, including Pier I, which offers imported glassware in an ever changing variety of styles; and Crate and Barrel and Williams-Sonoma, two wonderful stores for cooks who like to browse. Both of them also do mail-order business and are included in that listing. In addition, Williams-Sonoma operates a franchised store called Hold Everything, which features containers of all sorts, from closet components to cassette holders, with a few possibilities for containing gifts of food.

Oh, and don't overlook the mall. Check craft and hobby shops, beauty supply houses, and, of course, cooking-gear places for containers and trimmings. Even hardware stores and those gigantic discount emporiums can yield a surprising selection of container possibilities.

As for mail-order suppliers, a few can provide unique vessels for packing up food. Some are listed here.

American Spoon Foods, Inc.
P.O. Box 566
Petoskey, MI 49770-0566
Phone: 616-347-9030/800-222-5886
Fax: 616-347-2512

While it's chiefly a purveyor of gourmet foods, American Spoon does sell a line of one-of-a-kind handmade baskets, made by a family in Michigan's Upper Peninsula using bark harvested from fallen birch trees. They come in several sizes and make great one-of-a-kind gift containers that can be recycled into plant holders or seasonal centerpieces.

Chamomile Farms, Inc.
760 W. Hampshire Blvd.
Citrus Springs, FL 34434
Phone: 800-548-1592

A nice selection of baskets is found here, plus some other interesting possibilities for gifts to give with food: a specially designed pâté crock and spreader, spice grinders, and little muslin bags that would work perfectly for some of the seasoning mixtures described in chapter 7.

The Caning Shop
926 Gilman St.
Berkeley, CA 94710
Phone: 800-544-3374

Intended for chair and basket makers, this catalog has a wide assortment of supplies and reading material related to homemade basketmaking.

Chef's Catalog
3215 Commercial Ave.
Northbrook, IL 60062-1900
Phone: 800-338-3232
Fax: 708-480-8929

A great wish book for cooks, this catalog includes a few containers and baskets, and some possibilities for carriers, including a deluxe copper party tub designed to cool bottles of wine.

Crate and Barrel
P.O. Box 9059
Wheeling, IL 60090-9059
Phone: 800-323-5461
Fax: 708-215-0482

Simple, classic designs predominate in this striking catalog. Because the stock depicted changes from one issue to the next, it might be difficult to find the variety of containers that are available in the store's regular retail outlets, but you always can ask the operator about availability of nonpictured vessels when you call.

GH Productions-LF
521 E. Walnut St.
Scottsville, KY 42164

To carry the "handmade" theme to the hilt, consider weaving a basket to carry the sumptuous goods. This address can furnish you with a catalog of supplies for the basket maker, whether you're a neophyte weaver of straw or an old hand.

Hold Everything
100 North Point (Attn. Hold Everything catalog department)
San Francisco, CA 94133
Phone: 800-421-2264
A nationally distributed chain with 38 retail outlets, this company specializes in closet organizing equipment and storage units.

Home Canning Supply & Specialties
P.O. Box 1158-H7
Ramona, CA 92065
This no-nonsense catalog offers jars and all their trimmings, plus spices, pectin, and other necessities for putting up the harvest.

Home-Sew
P.O. Box 4099
Bethlehem, PA 18018-0099
Phone: 215-867-3833
Fax: 215-867-9717
Everything for the craft-inclined home sewer is in this catalog, including a variety of trims, laces, and buttons. Paper raffia also is shown, in a selection of colors, as well as a collection of band boxes in nesting sizes, which would make perfect, easy-to-decorate food containers.

Imagine That
1173 W. Country Creek Dr.
South Jordan, UT 84065
Phone: 801-254-1538
Rubber stamps for every occasion and sentiment are available here, plus non-message images from dancing hearts to cute little baby chicks and bunnies to several borders that would be perfect for making gift tags. There's even a stamp that reads "Made with love."

Kimberly Novelty Fabrics & Notions
P. O. Box 8006
Central Valley, CA 96019
Phone: 800-638-7491
Fancy touches can be found in here, like bits of elaborate lace and several kinds of patterned tulle. If you really want to go for the glitz, check out the sequined appliques, rhinestone buttons, and pearl-studded lacy things.

Kitchen Krafts
P.O. Box 805
Mt. Laurel, NJ 08054
Phone: 800-776-0575
A true wish book for the baker, this catalog features lots of fascinating gear for preparing food of all sorts. There are liqueur/vinegar bottles, gifts tags and jar labels, boxes for packing food, candy molds, and kitchen gadgets galore. And there are plenty of possibilities for companion presents to pack along with food gifts.

Lillian Vernon Corp.
Virginia Beach, VA 23479-0002
Phone: 804-430-1500
The attractive catalog sent by "Lillian" includes a variety of serving pieces and cooking utensils, many of which make good companion gifts to homemade foods, as well as baskets, tins, bottles, and jars.

Sunshine Discount Crafts
1280 N. Missouri Ave.
Largo, FL 34640
Phone: 813-581-1153
This all-purpose crafts catalog offers lots of ideas for embellishing gifts: cut blocks for printing with paint, stencils, bells, feathers, beads, decorative paints applied from squeeze bottles, and plenty more.

Williams-Sonoma
P.O. Box 7456
San Francisco, CA 94120-7456
Phone: 800-541-2233
This cooks' gear catalog includes assorted items with containing and/or packaging potential, including baskets, jars, and bottles.

Acknowledgments

Much assistance was lent to the making of this book. One might say that it is itself a product of gifts—the gifts of encouragement, constructive review, and inspiration.

On a most basic level I am indebted to my relations, a collection of people both far-flung and close-knit, the sort of group for whom the term *family* was invented. These people always have given me the feeling that there was absolutely nothing I couldn't do if I tried hard enough.

Specifically, I'm grateful to my sister and her husband, Melissa and Bill Oakley, and my husband, Dan, who tasted much of this stuff carefully and told me what they thought. Their careful and conscientious opinions gave me a needed sense of perspective. (My children, Erin, Sam, and Molly, whom I adore with all of my being, were loath to touch much of this stuff, being programmed sometime during toddlerhood to resist with all of their might things with names like *chutney* and *mustard* and *pesto.*)

Also due plenty of credit are my editor, Amy Teschner, whose inspiration, encouragement, and patience gave much of the impetus needed for this task, and her colleagues, who worked so deftly together to make the cover of this volume so enticing. One shouldn't judge a book by its cover, I know, but in this case, I hope one will.

Finally, and certainly not least significantly, I owe deep gratitude to a guy named Jesus, who reminded us all how very blessed this business of giving can be, and to His dad, whose grace makes all things possible.

Index